D0464020

THE
DIVINE
CONNECTION

THE DIVINE CONNECTION

*Understanding Your
Inherent Worth*

Lloyd D. Newell

Deseret Book Company
Salt Lake City, Utah

© 1992 Lloyd D. Newell

All rights reserved. No part of this book may be reproduced in any form or by any means without permission in writing from the publisher, Deseret Book Company, P.O. Box 30178, Salt Lake City, Utah 84130. This work is not an official publication of The Church of Jesus Christ of Latter-day Saints. The views expressed herein are the responsibility of the author and do not necessarily represent the position of the Church or of Deseret Book Company.

Deseret Book is a registered trademark of Deseret Book Company.

Library of Congress Cataloging-in-Publication Data

Newell, Lloyd D., 1956–
    The divine connection: understanding your inherent worth / Lloyd D. Newell.
      p. cm.
    Includes bibliographical references and index.
    ISBN 0-87579-645-1
    1. Self-respect—Religious aspects—Mormon Church 2. Christian life—Mormon authors. I. Title.
BX8656.N485   1992
248.4'89332—dc20   92-33191
                                        CIP

Printed in the United States of America

10   9   8   7   6   5   4   3   2   1

To Dad and Mom

CONTENTS

PREFACE

This is not a self-improvement book in the traditional sense. It is an *improvement* book, for certain, but it goes much deeper than what most of us know as *self*-improvement. We might even say that it takes the "self" out of "self-improvement."

Unlike many of the popular philosophies with which we are all familiar, this book emphasizes a faith in God rather than a reliance on self. Elder Jeffrey R. Holland explained that one of the biggest problems with modern society is its preoccupation with self, "self only — one life wide, and one life deep." We face the threat of "everyone getting in touch with himself at the expense of getting in touch with anyone else. . . . We live in a time in which there has been almost transcendent self-attention, in which the conquest of nature and search for new frontiers, social and otherwise, has given way to . . . 'self-realization.' "[1] Faith in God has, in many ways, been replaced with faith in human intellect, human achievement, human ability, or human potential.

But real power comes when we make a divine connection

to personal and interpersonal development, when our progress reflects a God-given and infinite potential. God-fearing believers have lived by such creeds through the ages. Jeremiah warned the Israelites, "Cursed be the man that trusteth in man, and maketh flesh his arm." (Jeremiah 17:5.) And Jesus explained: "That which is born of the flesh is flesh; and that which is born of the Spirit is spirit. Marvel not that I said unto thee, Ye must be born again." (John 3:6–7.) Part of the spiritual rebirth that Christ prescribes for us is what this book attempts to articulate. While using the language of self ("self-esteem," "self-improvement," and so on), the book is anything but selfish, and entirely against self-aggrandizement. It tells of the significant and even transforming change that a realization of our self-worth, or of our divine nature, can incite. Such an understanding of who we really are opens the door of selfless service, inspires us to make meaningful contributions to humanity, humbles us with gratitude, and helps us to see ourselves through a divine viewfinder of infinite potential. Indeed, the way we see ourselves and the world around us will never be quite the same.

The French writer André Gide wisely observed, "We cannot discover new oceans unless we have the courage to lose sight of the shore." As we turn the pages of this book, let us lose sight of the shores of human dependence (or traditional self-help wisdom) and explore the divine connection to progress that awaits our discovery. May we go forth with courage and faith to gain a deep understanding of our inherent and infinite worth.

ACKNOWLEDGMENTS

How can a first-time author adequately thank all the people who have helped him create a book — a book that has been in the works for many years?

This book reflects the greatness of people who have inspired and instructed me throughout my life, many of whom I know and others of whom I don't know. I believe that every experience of life becomes a part of how we live and think and feel: how we believe. And I thank the thousands of people I have met all over the world whose stories teach me, inspire me, entertain me, humble me, and have become a part of me. I also thank all of those who have been waiting for a book from me, who have encouraged me with their anticipation.

Sincere gratitude is extended to my publisher, Deseret Book Company, and its dedicated staff: Sheri Dew, Jack Lyon, Richard Erickson, Craig Geertsen, and Tonya Facemyer, who have offered valuable assistance and believed wholeheartedly in this book and its message. A special thanks to each of them and to Larry Morris for his editorial help.

Especially to my parents, to whom this book is dedicated, I offer my gratitude for their loving example of Christian living and service. And to my brothers and sisters, friends, and associates from whom I have gained great strength and insight through the years, I say thank you. I also appreciate the love and support from the Larry and Ruby Howell family.

Finally, to my wife, Karmel, who has powerfully believed in me from our first meeting, I give my deepest appreciation and love. Her assistance and enthusiasm and confidence in this project have helped make it possible and pleasurable.

. . . .

THE DIVINE CONNECTION

We are children of God.
And because of our divine connection,
we have inherent and unchanging worth.

CHAPTER 1

THE POWER OF SELF-WORTH

What lies behind us and what lies before us are tiny matters compared to what lies within us.
— Oliver Wendell Holmes

Much has been said about self-esteem in recent years. If you go to a bookstore and check the "Self-help," "Psychology," "Home and Family," or even the "Business" section, you will find scores of books on how to maximize personal and professional effectiveness with a properly developed, "new and improved" self-concept. Seminars by the hundreds saturate our psyches with self-improvement ideology. Articles on self-esteem and self-image spot nearly every periodical on the shelves; from *Forbes* to *Family Circle* to *Seventeen* to *Self*, magazines indoctrinate us with self-esteem psychology. An article on self-esteem in *Newsweek*, "Hey, I'm Terrific," documented: "A recent survey of the literature estimated that more than 10,000 scientific studies of self-esteem have been conducted. Researchers have measured it with more than 200 different tests."[1] Textbooks — replete with such testing — entertain the subject in all of its "scientific" depth, just as entire college courses are devoted to its discussion. Motivational audio and video tapes bring such self-improvement theories into our cars, businesses, exercise rooms, and homes.

Without question, self-esteem has become both a conversational and a clinical "cure-all," a catchword for the infirmities of our time. Almost every contemporary problem seems to hinge around self-concept; and many emotional, spiritual, and sometimes even physical ailments share the same diagnosis: poor self-esteem. What do our parents tell us about the neighborhood bullies? "They do not like themselves." Why do friends and co-workers misbehave? "Because they feel insecure and inadequate." And how are spouses able to mistreat their cherished companions? "By letting a poor self-image get in the way of real communication and selfless love." Such a correspondence between the private and the public, between liking ourselves before we can really like others, is a maxim from which both professional and pop psychologists draw many conclusions — and make many therapeutic suggestions. And rightly so.

Self-Worth vs. Self-Esteem

But let's take a step back to something even more fundamental. In our eager efforts to improve, sometimes the most basic ingredient for real improvement is neglected: a deep and meaningful realization of our divine connection — our relationship with God. How does self-worth differ from self-esteem, and why can an understanding of this difference ultimately change the way we live? Or perhaps more basic than these questions: Why is the topic of self-worth only superficially — and usually interchangeably — connected with self-esteem? Why does success literature lose self-worth to self-esteem? And how could the inclusion of this difference enhance the self-improvement material that already colors our shelves and illuminates our conversations?

Perhaps the best way I can explain the difference between self-worth and self-esteem (or even explain what self-worth is in the first place) is to review my own process of discovery. Nearly all the self-improvement books I have read and the tapes I have listened to place self-esteem at the center of self-help, declare positive thinking as an essential requirement for all change, and use self-worth as a synonym for self-esteem. I would not speak about self-esteem so regularly and study self-improvement literature so intensely if I did not sincerely believe in the importance of a healthy self-esteem, in the power of positive thinking, and in our capacity to change. Certainly, I do not discount such philosophies. Yet my studies have frequently left me feeling that something essential is missing, something intrinsic to the definition of self-worth, something deeply embedded in my own orientation for success that somehow eludes more widespread recognition.

I consciously realized this while searching the dictionary for just the right "self" word — and not being able to find it. *Self-worth* — that was the word I was looking for. But it was nowhere to be found. Of course, the usual "self" words were there: *self-concept*, *self-esteem*, and *self-image*. There are more than five hundred "self" entries in Webster's unabridged dictionary: *self-control*, *self-improvement*, *self-pity*, *self-respect*, *self-starter*, *self-winding*, *self-worship* — all kinds of entries ranging from *self-abandoned* to *self-wrong*, but not a single definition for *self-worth*.[2] Even in the twenty-volume

Oxford English Dictionary (which catalogues words from their origins to their current usages), *self-worth* was not to be found. *Self* was there and *worth* was there, but *self-worth* was not.

While searching for this elusive word, I was reminded of the transcendent truth I had been taught as a child: each of us is a child of God, and because of that, we all have infinite and eternal worth. Beyond mere self-esteem, a recognition of our inherent, divine endowment of value is the key to making real self-improvement. This is more than just a belief in ourselves; it is an acknowledgment of our divine value as unique human beings, as well as an acknowledgment of the eternal worth of every human soul.

The Divine Connection to Self-Improvement

This "oversight" became a perfect model for the sacred insight I had been attempting to articulate: more essential than good self-esteem is a recognition of our worth as children of God—and yet we seem to forget this basic truth in the very effort to enhance our perceived worth. Our search for self-esteem sometimes obscures our vision of inherent worth.

For example, if daily running becomes an obsessive ritual rather than a fulfilling exercise, we may really be running away from ourselves. Every time we look in the mirror, we will fail to see the exercised body before us for the ever-better body that could be ours. Our level of fitness will never be good enough when self-improvement has evolved into self-worship. The same idea applies to wealth and possessions when they lead to greedy acquisitiveness, for we can never get enough of what we don't need.

Similarly, if the wisdom we glean from reading becomes a principal source of self-identification, we will never be satisfied with the amount of knowledge we are acquiring. But when our identity is separate from any amount of learning we may aspire to, any wealth we may acquire, or any exercise we may follow; *when we know who we are* without having to show what we know, what we have, and what we can do; then reading, working, and running are the worthy self-improvements they should be. Such activities do not — and cannot — add to or subtract from our self-worth (our inherent value). They can only enhance our self-esteem (the way we feel about ourselves).

When we equate our self-esteem only with our efforts to improve, our self-evaluation becomes a superficial snapshot rather than a penetrating picture guided by a divine viewfinder. Only when the lens of improvement is brought into the focus of God-given worth does real progress and understanding take place. Only then does self-worth become the meaningful, even transformational, means and motivation for improvement that it should be.

The simple truth that we are children of a loving Heavenly Father is, for some, so obvious that it is sometimes discounted as too trite, too fundamental, and even too "religious" to be used in academic circles. We look to more "sophisticated" methods of measuring our identity. We may wear mood rings, take personality profiles, count calories, pay for "wellness consulting," and hover over horoscopes in order to find out about ourselves. But sometimes in the process, we lose sight of our eternal and internal identity. We may spend hours taking a test to determine what kind of a person we are, but rarely do we take a moment to reflect on the fact that we are literally children of God.

Public and private organizations may spend thousands of dollars for motivational training and personal improvement programs but never capitalize on the priceless — and perhaps single most motivating — truth that each of us has a divine inheritance of worth. We can become so energetic in our quest for personal success that, in practice, we may disconnect ourselves from the Greatest Energy Source, the Well-Spring of Success. We may become so focused on the "self" that we inadvertently forget Him who sustains us in our improvement, the Great Improver, through whom we *can* grow, change, and develop.

The more I thought about the emblematic oversight of *self-worth* in the dictionary, the more I realized a neglect of *self-worth* in most books' indexes. I reflected on certain frustrations I have had as a student of self-esteem literature and as a professor of self-help philosophy, and I was able to attribute these concerns to the absence of this divine connection to self-esteem. The self-help books and tapes with which I was familiar outlined great ideas and philosophies for improvement without any recognition or reliance on God. They were so "self-centered" there was no room for a Divine Center. And, in the end, a guiding principle for self-improvement became glaringly apparent to me. The widespread theories on selfhood and a personal desire to involve the Lord in a quest for improvement did not have to be mutually exclusive. In fact, a recognition of our self-worth would enhance every effort to improve our self-esteem because it would put an awareness of our God-given worth back into the self-improvement theories that already make our lives more meaningful.

The molding of our characters, bodies, and even our life-styles would be more complete if our efforts to improve were guided by the refining conviction that each of us is a child of God. Such an understanding of our heavenly heritage instills a deep sense of stewardship about everything in life. When we sincerely believe that we are God's children, we also realize that our time, talents, possessions, relationships, and even our physical bodies are not just our own. We treat everything from the earth to her creatures to our associates and even ourselves differently when we recognize this truth. We are on God's errand; we are His earthly stewards, managing the responsibilities and opportunities with which we are each endowed. And because we are stewards rather than servants, we not only care for the gifts we have, but we also feel a certain ownership over them. Indeed, the implications of this personal ownership are far-reaching for those committed to self-improvement.

What Does It Mean to Be a Child of God?

An understanding of the exalting truth that each of us has a divine inheritance of worth will enrich every effort we make to improve ourselves. Whether it be a social, intellectual, spiritual, or even a physical plan for progress, self-improvement becomes personal empowerment when guided by the recognition that we are children of a loving Heavenly Father. Perhaps the best way to make such a lofty truth more tangible is to consider what it means to be a child of earthly parents — or, quite simply, what it means to be a child. Why is there an eternal cycle of children growing into parents and parents having children?

I am the son of Neil and Verna Newell, and that means I carry on their names, inherit many of their characteristics, and continue their values (to varying degrees). No matter how mature and sophisticated I may become, I will always be their child. I am connected to them by virtue of my birth. Even as a father or grandfather, I will always be their son. In some ways, I will always be dependent on them. While this reliance originally took the form of physical provision and comfort, it has evolved into more of an emotional, and even a spiritual, support. I go to them for advice and look to them for a certain amount of unconditional acceptance and love. Even though my father has passed away, I am still encircled by both his and my mother's eternal stewardship.

Applying this childlike dependence to our relationship with God shows that we have not only a divine birthright but also the ability — and even the responsibility — to involve the Lord in our lives. Although the child in each of us occasionally disguises itself with costumes of experience or robes of knowledge, somewhere beneath all those hard-won layers (awarded by the "school of hard knocks") is a child — a child who is just like all other children: naturally teachable, essentially dependent, alarmingly discerning, and unconditionally loving. If this child seems buried in times of trial and periods of pain, we can renew our spirits by observing a child. Such observation leads to illuminating truths about our eternal childhood. A gaze through this carefully focused lens allows us to see the fine but immutably inscribed print on each of our birth certificates: *"You are of infinite and individual worth. You are the essence of greatness with divine and unlimited potential. You are a child of God."* And because of that, we each have a perfectly paved (but not necessarily easy) road for success. We need only humble ourselves, like a child, so that we can be led, guided, and walked beside on that personalized path for progress. Perhaps even more humbling, we have to believe in and ask for God's redeeming help when we can no longer pick ourselves up from the unavoidable stumbling blocks along the way.

The Savior becomes our catalyst for improvement when we recognize not only our need to change but also our childlike dependence upon Him. The words of a beloved song from childhood are perhaps most effective in conveying this message:

> I am a child of God, and He has sent me here,
> Has given me an earthly home with parents kind and
> dear.
> Lead me, guide me, walk beside me, help me find the
> way.
> Teach me all that I must do to live with Him some-
> day.[3]

Our Eternal Worth

We cannot get more worth. A larger house, a better salary, and an impressive investment portfolio may give us more net worth, but our self-worth remains constant. Getting a new job or not getting a new job, driving an expensive car or driving a used car, wearing new clothes or putting on old clothes will not affect our self-worth, either positively or negatively. While our self-esteem fluctuates, our self-worth never changes. Our *feelings* of self-worth (or the degree to which an understanding of our self-worth is deeply internalized) will vary; but unlike self-esteem, our self-worth is unaffected by the ups and downs of life. It is a constant power and comfort in our lives. *We* change as we recognize — and act upon — this inherent gift, this endowment from God. But our self-worth is always the same. The more we realize our intrinsic worth, the less our self-esteem fluctuates, the more we are empowered to change our lives and build our self-esteem.

There is no greater demonstration of both our individual worth and our ability to change than Christ's atonement. I remember a recent conversation I had to this effect. Some associates and I were discussing the idea of self-worth after a seminar one day. One of them interrupted our conversation and challenged, "But do hardened criminals have the same worth as the person who has lived a more reputable and moral life?" Before I had a chance to respond, another friend poignantly replied, "Yes. They have so much worth that Christ died on the cross — even for them." And I could only nod my head in humble agreement.

Each of us has such intrinsic worth that even those who commit heinous crimes can draw upon this divine inheritance of worth and work change in their lives. Paul explained this principle to the Romans hundreds of years ago: "God commendeth his love toward us, in that, while we were yet sinners, Christ died for us." (Romans 5:8.) What greater demonstration of both love and hope is there than that Christ would not just die for us, but, as Paul says, die believing in our ability to change — "while we were yet sinners." Paul similarly expressed to Timothy, "Christ Jesus came into the world to save sinners; of whom I am chief." (1 Timothy 1:15.)

Jesus is the Savior of the world, the Savior of saint and sinner alike. Each of us has an equal right to His saving sacrifice because each of us is of equal worth in His sight. The only prerequisite for calling upon such redeeming love is a childlike submissiveness that allows us to recognize not only our need to improve but also our inability to do so by ourselves. In the Savior's own words, we learn of the necessity for childlike humility: "Whosoever shall not receive the kingdom of God as a little child, he shall not enter therein." (Mark 10:15.)

Perhaps that is why the scriptures are replete with references to childhood. If we would incorporate childlike attitudes when we confront adult problems, we would draw upon our divine birthright to facilitate change. Isaiah prophesies that "a little child shall lead them" (Isaiah 11:6), and Hosea reveals that "when Israel was a child, then I loved him" (Hosea 11:1). In the same way, the Lord, in all of His glory, leads with meekness, "as a little child." Children, or at least childlike adults, are the object of God's greatest affection and blessing. Paul says it all in his epistle to the Romans: "The Spirit itself beareth witness with our spirit, that *we are children of God:* and if children, then heirs; heirs of God, and joint-heirs with Christ." (Romans 8:16–17.) Heirs of all the eternal worth and infinite value that a loving and omnipotent Father could instill in His own offspring,

we are each endowed with every right and every responsibility for self-improvement.

All of this brings us back to our leading questions: what
is the difference between self-worth and self-esteem? and
how can we derive power from a recognition of this difference? The answers to both queries are in our definition of
self-worth:

> Because I am a child of a loving God, I have inherent
> and infinite worth, and that understanding enables me
> to fulfill my unique potential, to value others' eternal
> worth, and, by so doing, to live an abundant life.

This definition will serve not only as the focus for this
book but, more important, as a guiding principle in all our
efforts to improve. When we realize that self-improvement
can neither add to nor take away from our individual worth,
we realize the untapped power in each of us. We experience
a quiet explosion of the divinity within us. And the more
we incorporate an understanding of our self-worth into our
plans for personal progress, the more meaningful and lasting
our efforts to improve will become.

· ·

THE ETERNAL NATURE
OF SELF-WORTH

We cannot get more worth.
While our self-esteem fluctuates,
our self-worth remains the same.

CHAPTER 2

THE SAVIOR'S DISCOURSE ON SELF-WORTH

Deep within the individual is a vast reservoir of untapped power waiting to be used. No person can have the use of all this potential until he learns to know his or her own self. The trouble with many people who fail is that they go through life thinking and writing themselves off as ordinary, commonplace persons. Having no proper belief in themselves, they fail to utilize their talents. They live aimless and erratic lives very largely because they never realize what their lives really can be or what they can become.

—Norman Vincent Peale

Self-improvement is central to Christian living. Christ's teachings are, in effect, a program for personal progress—a set of guidelines for right and for righteous living. Not only has Christ shown us the way to invoke change, but His atonement has made it possible for us to do so. While the atonement is a universal gift, we must make an active claim upon the Savior's sacrifice and teachings. As children of a God who loved the world so much that He gave his Only Begotten Son, we have the right—and even the responsibility—to embrace this redeeming love and allow the Lord to work a transformation in our lives. (See John 3:16.)

17

Transformation is the essence of Christianity: Christ died so that we might live anew, and, ultimately, so that we might achieve perfection, "even as [our] Father which is in heaven is perfect." (Matthew 5:48.) And in no way can we realize this perfection unless we recognize our self-worth, or our capacity to change coupled with our birthright of the Lord's unconditional love.

The Parable of the Prodigal Son

This truth is beautifully illustrated by the archetypal story of the prodigal son, which can be read as one of the Savior's discourses on self-worth. (See Luke 15:11–32.) The prodigal son's initial request for his inheritance merits careful scrutiny. He doesn't just ask for money upon leaving home, but he rather presumptuously demands, "Father, give me the portion of goods *that falleth to me.*" (V. 12; italics added.) It is an uncontested fact that an inheritance has been allocated to him. There is no question that certain of the goods "falleth to [him]" as one of his father's children — just as each of our divine inheritances of worth are unconditional endowments from God, gifts that have been freely given to all.

The prodigal son seems to recognize his worth, but he does so in a rather prideful way. As the parable illustrates, it is not enough to be aware of our inherent and infinite worth without simultaneously recognizing the Wellspring of that worth, or without humbling ourselves before God. The prodigal son's downfall is foreshadowed by the demanding nature of his request. He was aware of his promised inheritance, but by requiring of his father what was intended to be a gift, he began to mismanage and even lose sight of his generous reward. Remarkably, the prodigal son denies his worth even while he is in full possession of it—partly because he fails to honor the Source of his endowed strength.

The prodigal son then journeys to a far country and "waste[s] his substance with riotous living." (V. 13.) A famine plagues the land, and the boy begins to starve. Forced into humility by the pains of hunger and the sweat of menial labor, the son "would fain have filled his belly with the husks that the swine did eat." (V. 16.) Then comes a pivotal moment of truth: "And *when he came to himself*, he said, How many hired servants of my father's have bread enough and to spare, and I perish with hunger!" (V. 17; italics added.) The entire parable turns on the phrase "when he came to himself."

As if for the first time, the son humbly recognizes both his birthright as his father's son and his never-ceasing dependence upon him. His temporal birthright from an earthly father is an emblem of his (and of all humanity's) spiritual birthright from our Heavenly Father. In other words, it is a manifestation of his divinely endowed worth. And once he realizes this worth—once he "comes to himself"—he is able to initiate constructive change. Even though the son has regressive moments during the trek home when he questions his *worth*iness to be loved again, his father assuages all fear and doubt when he welcomes him back with a robe, ring, shoes, and festivities. And so it is with each of us. Our worth is constant, immeasurable, and unchanging. We need only "come to [ourselves]" so that the Lord's redeeming love can work in us and lead us along the pathway to perfection.

We are all prodigal children at one time or another in our lives. If only momentarily, we all lose sight of who we really are and make decisions that do not reflect our divinely invested worth. And by so doing, we lower our self-esteem.

While our worth remains constant, sometimes it takes a moment of reflection or an evening of celebration to remind ourselves that we are children of a loving God who wants us to live up to the greatness within us. Not only does the prodigal's father kill the fatted calf and organize a party on his son's behalf, but also, in the two related parables ("The Parable of the Lost Coin" and "The Parable of the Lost Sheep") that precede this story, the stewards have cause to make merry when they find their respective belongings, a piece of silver and a sheep. The shepherd "calleth together his friends and neighbours, saying unto them, Rejoice with me; for I have found my sheep which was lost." (V. 6.) Likewise, the woman who loses her coin "calleth her friends and her neighbours together, saying, Rejoice with me; for I have found the piece which I had lost." (V. 9.) In all three cases, the father, the shepherd, and the woman pause to celebrate their findings, or, we might say, they pause to recognize and celebrate the worth of those findings.

Celebrating Our Worth

There is something to be said for this kind of commemoration. Whether through an organized gala like those in the parables or even with just a minute of quiet contemplation, we would all glean strength from a purposeful re-

minder of our self-worth. By virtue of our birth, because
we all have birthdays, we are all entitled to "worth" days,
or at least hours or even moments when we pause to recognize our inherent worth. Whether or not we have celebrated these birthdays in the past does not change the fact
that we all have cause to celebrate — just because we were
born and because we are alive. We can make our next
birthday a "worth" day and, if only for a moment, remind
ourselves of the infinite worth that is God's gift to us (a gift
that truly keeps on giving).

Perhaps such worthy reflection would have eased the
jealousy of the prodigal's elder brother, who returns from
the fields only to hear music and dancing and merrymaking
on his brother's behalf. When the elder brother learns that
the festivities are in honor of his wayward brother, he resents
the celebration and refuses to enter the house. The father
comes out to persuade him to join the party, but the brother
fumes at his father, "Lo, these many years do I serve thee,
neither transgressed I at any time thy commandment: and
yet thou never gavest me a kid, that I might make merry
with my friends: but as soon as this thy son was come, which
hath devoured thy living with harlots, thou hast killed for
him the fatted calf." (Vv. 29–30.)

The brother seems to have lost sight of his worth; he
has forgotten the ever-present and unchanging value that
his father places upon him. Just as our Heavenly Father
never forgets who we really are, the father never loses sight
of either son's worth: "Son, thou art ever with me, and all
that I have is thine. It was meet that we should make merry,
and be glad: for this thy brother was dead, and is alive again;

and was lost, and is found." (Vv. 31–32.) Both the prodigal's and the elder son's worth never change; only their faithfulness, the degree to which they align their thoughts and actions with their worth, varies.

While each is equally valued, the elder brother is the more faithful. James E. Talmage explains in *Jesus the Christ:*

> We are not justified in extolling the virtue of repentance on the part of the prodigal above the faithful, plodding service of his brother, who had remained at home, true to the duties required of him. The devoted son was the heir; the father did not disparage his worth, nor deny his deserts. . . . There is no justification for the inference that a repentant sinner is to be given precedence over a righteous soul who had resisted sin; were such the way of God, then Christ, the one sinless Man, would be surpassed in the Father's esteem by regenerate offenders. Unqualifiedly offensive as is sin, the sinner is yet precious in the Father's eyes, because of the possibility of his repentance and return to righteousness.[1]

So while both the prodigal son and his elder brother were given an equal inheritance or a commensurate endowment of worth, the prodigal son had been less respectful of that inheritance (or worth) than his brother — even while both of their endowments remained constant. And just as the prodigal initially failed to recognize his value in his father's sight, perhaps the elder son would not have been so disgruntled by his brother's return had he been more fully aware of his own worth — as well as of his wayward brother's worth. Perhaps then the elder brother would have felt more secure about his own faithfulness and more willing to accept his brother as a fallible, changing person, in need of his forgiveness, love, and acceptance.

Lifted out of Darkness

Sometimes we require humbling experiences like this one to strip ourselves of superficial hallmarks of worth and really understand our self-worth. The simplest source of true worth, a recognition that we are children of God, can easily be lost to the more complicated demands of a "successful" life.

J. C. Penney, the wealthy entrepreneur and owner of more than sixteen hundred stores spotting almost every state, discovered his worth after losing almost all that he had. The Penney chain had survived the crash of 1929 and weathered the Depression reasonably well. Penney himself, however, had made some unwise personal investments before the crash and, like many other business executives, was blamed for events out of his control.

These worries began to wear on him physically, and, despite his wealth, he grew less sure of both his net worth and his self-worth. He became so troubled and nervous that he would go for days without sleeping. Eventually he contracted an extreme case of shingles (an excruciatingly painful skin rash) and was hospitalized. Medical treatment did not relieve him, however, and Penney's condition rapidly worsened. He relates: "I was broken nervously and physically, filled with despair, unable to see even a ray of hope. I had nothing to live for." Convinced that he would not see another sunrise, he wrote a farewell letter to his family and signed his name for what he thought would be the last time.

Despite his own doubts, Penney woke up the next morn-

ing to a new day—and a new orientation toward life. Surprised that he was even alive, he questioned his own hearing
when the melodic strains of a hymn found their way into
his hospital room. Intrigued by the fresh and somehow
familiar song, he struggled out of bed and followed the music
into the resident chapel. A group of patients was singing
the hymn "God Will Take Care of You," and Penney felt
that God was speaking directly to his heart. He also listened
to the reading of a scripture and bowed his head with the
congregation in prayer. Then something happened in his
soul. He later recalled: "I can only call it a miracle. I felt
as if I had been instantly lifted out of the darkness of a
dungeon into warm, brilliant sunshine. I felt as if I had
been transported from hell to paradise. I felt the power of
God as I had never felt it before."[2]

The Power of Transformation

Penney called it the most dramatic and glorious twenty
minutes of his life. The realization that God loved him
transformed him into a new person. Believing the words of
the hymn, he was empowered with a sense of worth and
was able to rediscover purpose in his life. God would take
care of him. And because he recognized that truth, he
experienced a rebirth. He "came to himself" and realized
that he possessed inherent value and was an heir to Godly
love. Like the prodigal son, he was dead and became alive;
he was lost and then lovingly found.

For J. C. Penney, for the prodigal son, and for each of
us, a recognition of self-worth is the key to personal transformation, to significant and lasting change. Just as the

popular toys called "transformers" can be altered by turning one hinge after another, we can control our lives by turning to God for help in adjusting the "movable parts" of our souls. My nephews carefully instructed me on the mechanisms of these innovative toys some years ago. They explained how one transformer could be changed from a pickup truck into a "good guy" by turning certain pieces and adjusting other parts, and another could be transformed from a cassette player into a "bad guy" through a similar evolutionary process.

The toys were rather illustrative of the Christian promise for change: each of us has the ability to transform our lives by making one small improvement after another in our character, personality, or even physical body. But just as we can make changes for the better, it is also possible to make wrong or unnecessary changes. Change for its own sake may not be desirable, but change that is guided by the knowledge of our God-given worth is the essence of Christian living.

Transformation does not take place in an instant. No matter how singular and life-changing an experience might be, transformation is a perpetual process of change, a series of consistent self-improvements. The Apostle Paul experienced one of the most dramatic transformations in the Bible, and yet it was in his day-to-day living that he worked a mighty and lasting change — by regularly adhering to one self-improvement after another. As Saul of Tarsus, he had been a vehement adversary to the Christian cause, "breathing out threatenings and slaughter against the disciples of the Lord" and even consenting to Stephen's death. (Acts

9:1.) But when Paul had a vision and heard the voice of the Lord, when he "came to himself," he saw himself through God's eyes and realized the unique mission he had to accomplish.

Once he realized that he was a "chosen vessel" who would suffer great things for the cause of righteousness, he used that divine connection to change his ways and to mold his missionary character. He took up the cause of Christianity with even more zeal than he had shown in opposing it because he now realized that he — and all of his fellow creatures — were the "offspring of God." (Acts 17:29.) Paul healed the lame, cast out devils, withstood stonings, converted congregations, and ultimately gave his life for the faith because he knew that God had spoken to him — and he sustained that knowledge through daily efforts to align his life with the mission revealed to him.

Transforming Events

While most of us will not have the kind of visitation that Paul had, all of us will — if we recognize them — undergo what can be called "transforming experiences." We need only keep our heart and mind open during these important and impressionable times. Whether they be a period of trial or an occasion for joy, transforming events are usually cloaked in the pedestrian apparel of the everyday. I will always remember a transformational experience I had in a quiet moment after my father's death.

Feelings of loneliness, bewilderment, and even despair were clouding my thoughts as I rummaged through some of my father's belongings with my now widowed mother. He had died a sudden, accidental death, and we were left no time to prepare for the most shocking news of our lives. In a numbed state of survivalistic acceptance, my mother turned to me with a sweater in her hands and a sliver of a smile on her face. She handed me the wool cardigan that I had given my father several years before — the sweater that he wore almost every day. As I opened its buttons and unfolded the creases in the sleeves, it seemed to exhale my father's memories. At first I was afraid to put it on. But when I finally slipped one arm in, the other arm seemed to fall naturally into place, and before long I felt empowered by its warmth. The sweater was a perfect fit from the first time I put it on.

I stood up and looked in the mirror, and I had what I would consider a transforming experience. In my mind's eye, I saw my father's countenance upon me. I saw my father in me, not just in the physical trappings of his old sweater but, more significantly, in the valuable inheritance he had left me: the love, values, example, and good name that were my birthright. Tears welled in my eyes, and empty longings were accompanied by a grateful heart. My father would never be lost to me. He had instilled in me a life of exemplary love and service, and, because of that, he would always be a part of me — or perhaps more accurately, I would always be a part of him. As his son, I could ever draw from his reservoir of strength and wear his mantle of worth upon my shoulders.

I still wear that sweater, and every time I look at it I am reminded of the priceless inheritance of love and Christian example and teachings my father gave me. In the same way that a recognition of the intangible inheritance I received from my earthly father eased my pain, a realization of the Lord's promise to each of us can give us the necessary fortitude to meet all worthy goals. The Savior has given a universal promise: "Take my yoke upon you, and learn of me; for I am meek and lowly in heart: and ye shall find rest unto your souls." (Matthew 11:29.) Because we are all children of God, we not only *can* take His yoke upon us, but, as His offspring, it is our birthright to do so. Each of us has a God-given "sweater," an inheritance of worth that is perfectly fitted to our person. And just as I was blessed with a peaceful assurance that I could meet the challenges before me when I put on my father's sweater, each of us is promised "rest unto [our] souls" when we take His yoke upon us: when we learn of Him and adopt His countenance.

Most frequently, we feel this transforming peace in unannounced, day-to-day interactions. A passing compliment, a breathtaking view, or a small act of service will remind us of the heavenly love and inherent worth to which we all have claim. After an exhausting day at work, a short message on my answering machine from my three-year-old nephew brought a smile to my face and filled my soul with untapped energy. "I love you, Noid; I miss you," is all that he said. But somehow he said more to me. His simple love spoke of the profound love that my Heavenly Father has for me—and for each of us.

Isn't it great to be alive? Something as simple as hearing a child's voice, watching a flock of birds play outside the window, listening to the leaves crunch underfoot on a cool autumn day, or feeling the sun's warm rays on our shoulders tells of the preciousness of life and the endowment of worth that God has given us. He cares about us so much that He has bestowed such priceless gifts as beautiful landscapes, cherished relationships, and divinely inspired scriptures to lead us back to Him.

Staying open to these daily manifestations of God's love will ready our hearts and minds for the kind of transformation that Christ envisioned when He challenged us, "Be ye . . . perfect." (Matthew 5:48.) This imperative statement is perhaps one of the greatest evidences of our inherent worth. So much is invested in and expected of us as God's children that we *can* eventually become like Him. Ultimately, whether in this life or in the next, we have what it takes to become perfect. C. S. Lewis bears a powerful testimony to this end in *Mere Christianity:*

> The command *Be ye perfect* is not idealistic gas. Nor is it a command to do the impossible. He is going to make us into creatures that can obey that command. He said [in the Bible] that we were "gods" and He is going to make good His words. If we let Him—for we can prevent Him, if we choose—He will make the feeblest and filthiest of us into a god or goddess, a dazzling, radiant, immortal creature, pulsating all through with such energy and joy and wisdom and love as we cannot now imagine, a bright stainless mirror which reflects back to God perfectly (though, of course, on a smaller scale) His own boundless power and delight and goodness. The process will be long and in parts very painful; but that is what we are in for. Nothing less. He meant what he said.[3]

And because He meant it when He said we should work

toward perfection, we can get a sense of the power that is within us to transform our lives. We can, in effect, "come to ourselves," or catch sight of the real deep-down, inside-the-skin you and me who are ever visible to our Heavenly Father. Through the grace of God, we can abandon old ways and ever see things anew.

The Potter's Wheel

In the same way that Jeremiah urged ancient Israel to become "as the clay is in the potter's hand," to become malleable to change, each of us can best improve ourselves by looking to God to mold our lives. (Jeremiah 18:6.) We are the clay. He is the Master Potter who lovingly shapes us and smooths out the rough places in our character. We need only be humble enough to change and to see His handiwork in the small acts of wonder that are daily before us.

By so doing, we will steadily evolve into the sculpted masterpiece that we are meant to be. I was struck by some poignant words to this effect from an older woman in a seminar I was conducting. During the middle of the presentation, she raised her hand and with a feeble but resonant voice said, "I'm a masterpiece in progress—I'm not done yet!" Could there be a truer statement?

We are all masterpieces in progress, clay in God's hands, worthy of the molding, sculpting, and scraping that life affords us. We all have the seeds of godhood in us, and in no better way do we let these seeds germinate and grow than when we "come to ourselves" by realizing our self-worth and allowing for a process of godly transformation.

President David O. McKay wrote: "Sculptors of life are we, with our uncarved souls before us. Every one of us is carving a soul. Is it going to be a deformed one or is it going to be a thing of beauty?"[4]

The earth and all of its creatures bespeak such change. As Jesus said of the mustard seed, "[It] is the least of all seeds: but when it is grown, it is the greatest among herbs, and becometh a tree, so that the birds of the air come and lodge in the branches thereof." (Matthew 13:32.) Like the mustard seed, we are all growing, and we can work a mighty change and transform our lives. When we sincerely desire to realize our God-given capabilities — when we deeply realize our self-worth — we will humble ourselves, trust the Lord, and live up to the worthy aspirations that are ours to enjoy. We all stand with feet of clay. Each of us is subject to the throws of the Potter's wheel. And if we will hold fast to the inheritance of worth that is our birthright, we will become the masterwork that God intends us to be.

CHAPTER 3

VALUES AND THE DIVINE CONNECTION

> It is essential that the student acquire an understanding of and a lively feeling for values. [You] must acquire a vivid sense of the beautiful and of the morally good. Otherwise [you]—with [your] specialized knowledge—more closely resemble a well-trained dog than a harmoniously developed person.
>
> —Albert Einstein

Each of us perceives the world, other people, and ourselves in a unique way. We may all look at the same person, thing, or situation, and see it very differently from each other because our experiences and backgrounds have created a personalized set of values for us. We all look at the world through a unique, even "customized," lens that is distinctly fashioned from our individual values. And because we each see the world through our own estimations of worth and worthiness, real self-perception involves not only a look at ourselves but also *at the lens through which we see*—at our set of values. What dimensions are the focal point of our viewfinder? From what vantage point do we usually take our pictures? What is our method of "capturing" the world?

Such clarification of our values is essential in making

meaningful change. Without stopping to examine the lens through which we view the world, we have no way of determining if our self-perceptions include all that they could and should—and if they exclude misconceptions that may weaken our resolve and damage our self-esteem. Sometimes we focus on outward appearance instead of inward substance and never get the "real" picture. We may be vogue on the outside and vague on the inside. Does our view of ourselves and of the world include an eternal perspective of God-given worth?

Transformation, the process of making significant change, is best guided by an awareness of who we really are—not just of who we perceive ourselves to be. If we can somehow remove ourselves from the distractions of life's photo session and concentrate on our *true* nature, we can make the necessary changes to align our life's lens with the Lord's all-seeing eye. Instead of seeing through our own restricted and imperfect viewfinder, we can open our understanding to the panoramic and eternal focus of a divine viewfinder. Such a realization will not only transform the way we see ourselves, our relationships, and the world, but it will even transform our very souls.

A Correct Map

Another useful way to explain this is to compare values with maps. If we lived our lives without realizing that we are children of a loving God, our search for meaning would be like traveling life's journey with an imperfect map. We would not know where we come from, where we presently stand, or where we are going. Why? Because we would not be able to see past the imperfections of our map and into the real, customized territory the Lord has prepared for each of us. We must remember that the man-made map (our self-esteem) is not the God-given territory (our self-worth). When we see ourselves as God sees us (as one of His children with infinite worth), not only do we alter our map so that our values reflect our worth, but we also catch sight of the wonders of the territory and realize the untapped wealth of resources that have been invested in us all along the way.

As one who has spent a good deal of time on the road, I can attest to the value of a good map. Without such a guide, traveling can be difficult. I remember driving on a lonely road in the dark of Alaska's heartland, uncertain about where I was but knowing I needed to find a remote lodge where I would be speaking the next morning. I was in a hurry. I thought I had no time to plan and prepare — no time to look at a map, let alone purchase one.

As a result, I had only a vague sense of where I should be going. After circling and searching well into the night, I determined never again to embark on such a journey without a better mapping of the course. No matter how positive my attitude and how strong my resolve to find my destination, my efforts were futile. (I reached my destination only after stopping to ask for directions.)

On another occasion, in Australia, I followed the markings of a good map but failed to make the necessary mental adjustments for driving on the left side of the road. This time, even though I had a map, because I was not following it correctly I had a few unnecessary detours — and even some close calls.

These instances of anxious searching are akin to the uncertainty we experience when we fail to clarify our values — when we fail to make a correct map and follow it, when we fail to realize our unchanging worth. Sometimes we are in such a hurry, we are so busy *going,* that we do not clarify where we are headed or how we are going to get there. We are busy being busy. We push the gas pedal clear to the floor, but our hands are not on the steering wheel.

Values give direction to our life's journey. They help us control our destiny by putting our hands on the steering wheel of life and our feet on the pedals of personal progress. Denis Waitley describes such a scenario: "If you don't know where you're going, you'll end up somewhere else, but it doesn't matter, because you don't recognize where you've been or where you are anyway."[1]

The Search for Values

In a society where uncertainty and confusion are not only accepted but even encouraged, values are frequently equated with societal norms, and moral instruction is — in many cases — left to the media. Everything from television programs to magazine ads to cereal boxes seems to push a set of values at us. Soap operas and sitcoms provide us with as many different pictures of life and "real" living as we are willing to buy into. We need only press a button to tune into the mode of living that would validate any life-style — however moral or immoral it may be. If we are looking for laziness, dishonesty, extravagance, sarcasm, or sexual immorality, we can find it at the push of a button.

Similarly, advertisers spare no expense to create "suc-

cess" images in attractive detail: on one channel happiness
is personified as a trim body that glides across a crowded
room of envious onlookers; on another, a full head of perfectly colored hair is the well-spring of joy; on yet another
channel, happiness is a cold glass of beer and a shiny new
car. One ad says that "everyone is doing it," even while
the "it" that everyone is doing may well be a description
of fleeting happiness and ill-defined morality, an "it" that is
changing from day to day. Few ads question whether or not
the popular way is the right way. Most often, they suggest
that what we *have* is more important than who we *are*, and,
as a result, clearly defined moral values are muddied by the
deceptive (but appealing) pollutants of status, wealth, and
possessions. Remember the popular comedian's famous line
from a few years ago? "It's better to *look* good—than to *be*
good."

Certainly, not everything on television or in a magazine
is abhorrent and deceptive. The media provide much valuable entertainment and learning. But as Dan Coats, a U.S.
senator from Indiana, says in his discourse "America's
Youth: Crisis of Character," the media has (for too many
children and adults) replaced moral instruction. And values
have been relegated to an informal and mostly unsupervised
education. The senator explains: "We live in a century in
which 'facts' are glorified while 'values' are assigned an
inferior status as mere matters of opinion. We have seen
the development of a militant relativism that dictates that
it is impossible to prefer one value above another, since all
conceptions of the good are equally subjective. . . . A public school survey in Maryland showed that parents spent an

average of 15 minutes a *week* in 'meaningful dialogue' with their children—children who are left to glean whatever values they can from peers and TV."[2]

For many youth—and even for many adults—the search for values has become a meaningless game of hide-and-seek. True and moral ways of doing things are confused by classifications of mere opinion. And immoral behavior is likewise subjected to relativism or "political correctness."

An article in *U.S. News and World Report,* "The Retro Campaign," showed similar findings: "About 8 in 10 Americans say they acquired their core values from the family, according to a new survey sponsored by Massachusetts Mutual Life Insurance Co. But two thirds say, unhappily, that today's children are getting their values from television, movies, musicians, or music videos."[3] More than ever before, with all the freedoms and opportunities before us, decision-making is complicated by ill-defined and even undefined guideposts of morality. A sociology professor at Rutgers, David Popenoe, characterizes our society in this way: "With all the pessimism and economic drift, people are looking around and asking what, after all, is most important in their lives."[4]

While looking in all directions for beacons of truth, we may fail to discover the lighthouse of worth within ourselves. But this need not be the case. Each of us has been given a priceless endowment that can direct our decisions and define our values.

The self-worth we have inherited as children of God is the territory against which we can chart our progress, a lens through which we can clarify our values, and a steering wheel with which we can confidently guide our course. Because we are the offspring of deity, our lives have meaning and purpose. We need only remember who we are and then make our decisions based upon this refining and redeeming awareness.

I remember a line to this effect from Wallace Stevens' poem "The Emperor of Ice-Cream": "Let be be finale of seem." I first read this poem quite a few years ago, and its message made an indelible mark in my mind: Don't just *seem*, but *be!* No matter what we may *seem* to be, we *are* (and always will be) children of God. While at times the reason for our being may elude us, our unique mission is ever-present to the Lord. Let be be finale of seem when it comes to the making of values.

Do You Want to Be a Success?

Many years ago while in college, I had to stop and take conscious inventory of my values. I had to step back from my mental "map-making" and make sure I was plotting the course in life I really wanted to take. While an awareness of my divine parentage was probably not as prevalent in my mind as the awareness that I had earthly parents who loved me and had shown me how to live happily, the same process of recognizing my worth and defining my priorities was put into play.

Working full-time and going to school full-time, I knew the value of a dollar. And so when I was offered a lucrative job selling a gas additive, a "miracle cure" that was supposed to dramatically increase a car's gas mileage (as well as my bank account), the prospect was appealing.

I heard the sales pitches and listened to the persuasive arguments, impressed that all of the founders *seemed* to be making huge sums of money — they all drove fancy cars and wore designer clothes and Rolex watches. At first, the questionable history of the company was all part of the intrigue. Some obscure researchers in the Midwest had formulated the breakthrough, and of course the "Big Three" automakers would be doing all in their power to suppress the discovery. I was led to believe that I was in on one of the greatest secrets in automotive history. But somehow it *seemed* too good to be true.

My interest began to deteriorate into mild irritation when one of the more persistent sales representatives visited me at work. He was trying to pressure me into a commitment. "Don't you want to be a success? Don't you want to have money? Don't you want to have a nice car like mine, dress like me, have an expensive watch like mine?" he challenged. Certainly these prospects were inviting for a poor student. But something about his standard for success seemed wrong, misguided. He continued to persuade with every imaginable attraction, and he became more animated as the list went on. He grew adamant, almost apoplectic, as he hovered over me with his red face and sweating brow.

Finally, I had endured enough. I conceded that I wanted to be a success, and I told him that I planned to be successful. But I was not going to let *him* define success for *me*. I told him about my father, who had little of what the world classifies as success: money, fame, power, and status. My father worked in a steel mill for thirty-seven years to provide for his wife and seven children. But he had an abundance of the things that really matter: loving relationships, earned respect, great spirituality, and a burning desire to learn and grow and serve. "Your fast-paced company," I told him, "may not survive the turn of the new year." (And it did not. Six months later it had completely folded.) But the kind of wealth my father possessed would bless countless generations.

The sales representative finally turned his head and walked toward the door, and I stood still for a minute, quietly pondering what had been a moment of truth for me. I had been backed up against the wall of decision, forced to clarify my values and act accordingly, and the greatest influence on my decision had been the example my father had given me. Because my parents had shown me the value of love and service and self-respect, I could make a choice that was in line with my inherent worth — and my *own* definition of success.

My father's strength was a type of the Universal Power to which we all have claim. The intangible inheritance my earthly parents gave me teaches me of the universal and eternal inheritance to which we all are heirs. A recognition that we have worth independent of all worldly measurements of value is the force behind all meaningful self-understanding and transformation. The Lord says it all when He asks: "What is a man profited, if he shall gain the whole world, and lose his own soul? or what shall a man give in exchange for his soul?" (Matthew 16:26.) The irreplacable wealth of divinely inspired, value-centered living puts all other life-styles (no matter how profitable they may be) into their proper, and sometimes meaningless, perspective. Real heart-and-soul satisfaction comes from aligning our lives with the people and things that matter most.

Who We Really Are

Acquiring an understanding of what matters most and of who we really are will help us to define our priorities, meet our aspirations, and uncover our unique purposes. When we realize that we are children of God, we know of the infinite and inherent capabilities we possess. This truth was poignantly expressed in the background music to a program that I was recording for teenagers. I was so struck by the message of the song that I wrote down the lyrics as I heard them:

> I've got to find out who I am,
> and when I do, I know I'll be all I can.
> When I find out who I am,
> I'll be all I can.

When we figure out who we are, what we're about, and what matters most to us, we can begin to become all that God intended us to be. No matter how well we think we know ourselves and our abilities, if we fail to deeply recognize that we are God's children, we will never fully realize our divine endowments. As Elder Neal Maxwell has said, "If we understand the basic purpose of life, we will find it easier to see purpose in our own life."[5]

Christ sets the perfect example of one who possessed this abiding sense of purpose. When Mary found the twelve-year-old Jesus after thinking He was lost somewhere in the streets of Jerusalem, He innocently responded to her questions: "How is it that ye sought me? wist ye not that I must be about my Father's business?" (Luke 2:49.) Jesus was so sure about His divine inheritance and His unique mission that He was puzzled that His mother would even wonder about His whereabouts. In His mind, He should not have been anywhere else but in the temple, His Father's house.

Jesus was so fully aware that God was His Father and that He had a mission to perform that, even as a child, He would naturally go to His Father's house. And throughout His life, when mobs combined, calumnies raged, and adversaries challenged, he replied, "Though I bear record of myself, yet my record is true: *for I know whence I came, and whither I go.*" (John 8:14; italics added.) Time and again, Jesus grounded His message and His life in the knowledge that He was sent from God with a saving mission.

And while Jesus is the Only Begotten Son of God, because each of us is God's child and because each of us has a unique mission to perform, we can find direction and purpose from this knowledge. When we base our values on this simple truth, not only does our life have more meaning, but the self-improvements we make will ultimately lead to the development of our God-given potential. We might well say that the process of life is realizing this potential: becoming who we really are and understanding what we are really about. Sometimes we are so busy making a living that we fail to design a life. And, as Goethe phrased it: "Things which matter most must never be at the mercy of things which matter least." But what are the things that matter most and least?

The Things That Matter Most

All too often a dramatic, soul-wrenching experience forces us to redefine our values. Unfortunately, sometimes that is all that will shake us up enough to realize that there is more to life than just living — or, for that matter, just making a living. Well-known CBS news reporter and Middle East correspondent Bob Simon provides an illuminating example of this phenomenon. As a former TV news anchor for a CBS affiliate myself, I have long admired Bob Simon and watched him as he has covered many major news stories. When war broke out with Iraq, it was not surprising to see Bob Simon at the front lines, sending all of the latest news home to anxious Americans. But then, unexpectedly, Bob Simon and his crew were taken prisoner, and for several weeks the rest of the world had no knowledge of whether they were alive or dead.

When the war ended, the good news of their survival was confirmed, and the war-weary prisoners were released. But Bob Simon and company had been affected by their unfavorable circumstances. They had been jolted out of a comfort zone of busy preoccupation. In an interview on "60 Minutes" shortly after his return, Mr. Simon described the soul-searching he had done, the value clarification in which he had engaged during this troublesome time. Instead of concerning himself with the big story, the journalistic possibilities, the history-making events, he had reflected on what mattered most to him during those days of subjugation. Freedom and liberty had become so precious. He had longed to have another walk along the beach with his daughter, another quiet conversation with his wife, another peaceful moment of contemplation. These were some of the things that really mattered to him. And the sense was that never again did he want to put them at the mercy of less valuable things.

Whether or not we undergo such a dramatic experience, all of us have cause to pause and decide what is most important to us — not what matters most to our friends, neighbors, or even family, but what means the most to *us*. And in no better way can we do this than by turning to God for direction and understanding.

I remember one such time upon graduating from college when I sought for guidance — and found it in the quiet recesses of my heart and mind. Ever since high school, I had been active in debate, public speaking, and student government. I had the "perfect portfolio" for entry into law school, and when I graduated with a bachelor's degree, it was only expected that I would go on to become a lawyer. I had taken the LSAT, filled out the applications, and readied myself for what seemed to be the next logical step in my life. By all exterior indicators, I was tailor-made for the profession.

But while I was waiting to hear from the law schools, something that had been gnawing inside of me for some time surfaced: I did not want to be a lawyer. My professors, my colleagues, and even some of my closest associates thought law was for me, but somehow I knew it wasn't. While law is a worthy profession, I had other interests and talents that I felt could be more fully cultivated by pursuing a graduate degree in communications. And after much prayer and introspection, I came to the peaceful assurance that this was the right decision for me.

Somehow my knowledge that there was a God in heaven to whom I could turn with weighty matters eased the decision-making process. And I felt at peace. I was better able to direct my life because I could rely on God's omniscience and know that He would guide me, as His son, to choose the more fulfilling path for me. Since that pivotal time in my life, I have looked back with many grateful sighs that I took an alternate route that was, for me, more closely aligned to what mattered most.

All of us redefine our values many times throughout our lives. But exactly how do we come to decide what matters most to us? How do we recognize what our values are? Perhaps one of the most effective ways to clarify our own fundamental beliefs and desires is to familiarize ourselves with other people's value systems. Whether it be through casual conversation, formal study, or directed listening, we can observe and evaluate others' beliefs so as to better formulate our own. For example, Napoleon Hill, author of the best-selling *Think and Grow Rich,* makes a thought-provoking list of "The Twelve Riches of Life," the values without which he believes one cannot be happy. He summarizes:

> 1. A Positive Mental Attitude: the starting point of all riches.
> 2. Sound Physical Health: results from positive thinking and balanced living.
> 3. Harmony in Human Relationships.
> 4. Freedom from Fear: no one who fears anything is a free human being.

5. The Hope of Achievement: poor beyond description is he who cannot look ahead with hope that he will still become the person he would like to be.

6. The Capacity for Faith: the connecting link between conscious mind and Infinite Intelligence.

7. Willingness to Share One's Blessings — which are multiplied by the simple process of sharing them where they may serve others.

8. A Labor of Love: engaging in it brings the joy of self-expression.

9. An Open Mind on All Subjects: only the tolerant mind becomes truly educated and thus prepared to enjoy all of life's riches.

10. Self-Discipline: mastery of self which leads to humility of heart.

11. The Capacity to Understand People: the foundation of all friendship, harmony, and cooperation among human people.

12. Economic Security: not attained by possession of money alone, but by the useful service one renders to others.[6]

While this list seems rather authoritative and all-inclusive, it is meant to be carefully considered — and challenged. This and all other value systems are relative determinations of worth, meant to inspire inquisitive minds and lead to the discovery of the unchanging *principles* and God-given *truths* behind such lists.

An Examined Life

There *is* a right and a wrong; there *is* a difference between truth and error. And the scriptures outline these differences for us. The Savior encouraged us to search for truth with the promise that "the truth shall make you free." (John

8:32.) He said of Himself and of His mission: "I am the way, the truth, and the life: no man cometh unto the Father, but by me." (John 14:6.)

The one and only way to our Heavenly Father is through His Son Jesus Christ. When we genuinely strive to live a Christian life, our values will conform to the truths that Christ taught — foremost of which is the understanding that He is our Savior, that He is God's Son, and that we are God's children. Since we all see things from a different perspective with our own customized lens of learning, no set of personal values may be exactly like another's. But when we are guided by the awareness that we have infinite and unchanging worth as children of God, that we are all the benefactors of Christ's redeeming sacrifice, our values will reflect saving principles and lead us to a personalized harvest of truth.

The first step toward such enlightenment is to characterize our present system of values. And building such an awareness is, in large measure, the object of this book. Most quick-and-easy lists or tests will not give us an entirely accurate evaluation of our values, but they may give us a sense of how we perceive the world. We need to take some pensive and prayerful time to come to such an understanding.

These seven questions may help us begin the value-clarifying process:

1. If I had a completely free year, how would I spend it? Would I work, play, spend time with family, write a book, read, travel, go back to school, sleep?

2. For whom or on what do I spend most of my money?

3. Why am I in my present occupation?

4. What would I most resist giving up?

5. Who are my role models—and why?

6. If I had only six months left to live, what would be most important to me? Would my values be different from what they are right now?

7. What words would I most like to be described by?

Also consider some typical values categories: personal, family, social, career, financial, community, and spiritual. List the categories in order of importance. Then write down what is most important to you in each area.

The answers to these questions and the hierarchy of such classifications are often difficult to determine. But as Plato said, "The life which is unexamined is not worth living." An honest investigation of our responses will lead to a better awareness of our values, and with this awareness we can make more meaningful decisions. Our whims will evolve into resolutions, and our goals will be guided by a value-centered vision. If not, we may spend all of our time and energy climbing to the top of a mountain and then realize that we have climbed the "wrong" mountain—a mountain for which we have no real affection or to which we attach little meaning. But when we clearly define our values before we begin the trek, our sincere efforts not only take us to the top of the mountain but also lead us up the "right" mountain, to our personalized pinnacle of success.

Only after we have paused to evaluate the lens through which we see ourselves and the world will we be able to discern which "mountain" really is best for us. Only then will we be able to determine if our lens is in need of repair, cleaning, or clarification. Only then will we be able to look to God for His panoramic vision. When our lens is free from the distracting influences of this world, when the light of Christ shines freely through it, we will uncover our inherent worth and draw upon the power of our divine heritage.

CHAPTER 4

OUR DIVINE PARENTAGE

I believe that I am a child of God, endowed with a divine
birthright. I believe that there is something of divinity
within me and within each of you. I believe that we have
a Godly inheritance and that it is our responsibility, our
obligation, and our opportunity to cultivate and nurture
the very best of these qualities within us.
—Gordon B. Hinckley

Popular self-improvement theory suggests that if you just
"believe in yourself," you can do anything. We are told
that everything is possible if we really put our minds to it.
Motivational speakers and writers promise us (ad infinitum)
that we need only believe, and then we will see whatever
it is we desire to accomplish. Much of the self-improvement
psychology is summarized in the well-known saying, "Whatever the mind can conceive and believe, the mind can
achieve." Such "believe-it-and-you'll-see-it" philosophy
certainly has its place and presents us with valid maxims.
Without question, positive thinking is a very real and powerful force.

But hundreds of years ago the Lord added upon such
positivism when He schooled His disciples in the doctrine
of salvation: "With men this is impossible; but with God

all things are possible." (Matthew 19:26.) Perhaps the allure of realizing that "all things *are* possible" has clouded our remembrance of the rest of the formula: "*with God,* all things are possible." In other words, while believing in ourselves is a worthy — and even necessary — mindset, by itself it is never enough.

No matter how thorough and visionary our goals and purposes may be, if they do not make a divine connection to success, all of our achievements may never fully represent our capabilities. Our external accomplishments may not reflect our internal, even eternal, possibilities. If we are really to believe in ourselves, we must first really believe in God.

The Power of Faith

So how do we begin to have such faith? Paul taught in his epistle to the Romans that faith can be kindled by hearing the testimonies of those who do believe: "So then faith cometh by hearing, and hearing by the word of God." (Romans 10:17.)

The faith-promoting story of Alice Alder, a Jew who survived the Holocaust, is sure to awaken such a God-fearing trust. Much like the more celebrated story of Victor Frankl (the Jewish prisoner who "thought" himself through the grueling captivity of a Nazi death camp and then told his stirring tale in his book *Man's Search for Meaning*), Alice Alder looked to God for physical, mental, and spiritual salvation. A thirty-one-year-old clothes designer and boutique owner in Hungary, Alice was enjoying a comfortable life-style when the Nazis invaded her homeland in 1944. Thrust from her thriving business and pleasant surroundings, she — along with many other Hungarian Jews — was forced into slave labor and moved from one concentration camp to another. Finally, she was put on a train bound for the gas chamber and the crematorium. An unquenchable belief that God had a purpose for her, however, gave Alice the necessary courage to leap from the train during a moment of welcome confusion — and save her life.

Injured, starving, and almost naked, Alice fought to survive in a strange land under uncertain circumstances. Eventually, a French partisan found her in this destitute condition and gave her the needed food and clothing to make a new start. Now in her seventies and living in America, Alice Alder looks back on that dark time through the illuminating lens of gratitude. She recognized then and glories now in the saving faith that carried her through: "I have always believed the hand of God was leading me. . . . I believe that somehow, somewhere, optimism and freedom will triumph."[1] Alice made a divine connection that enabled her to see beyond the confines of her captivity and into the freedoms of a God-centered life. She believed in her ability to accomplish the "impossible," because she knew that God had purpose for her and would help her to live up to her greatest possibilities. Alice was empowered by the recognition of her inherent, God-given worth.

In another country and a different century, the life of Abraham Lincoln also demonstrates the power that comes from faith. Born in a log cabin in the backwoods, Lincoln knew that God would help him to accomplish any worthy goal; he stopped at nothing to live up to his aspirations and help a struggling nation. His business failed in 1831; he was defeated when he ran for the legislature in 1832; his business failed again in 1834; his fiancée died in 1835; he was defeated in the election of 1838; he was defeated for Congress in 1843, in 1846, and again in 1848; he was defeated in the senate races of 1855 and 1858; and he was even defeated for the vice-presidency in 1856; yet he still ran for president *and was elected* in 1860!

But even that win was a marginal victory. The vote was split among four candidates: Bell, Breckinridge, Lincoln, and Lincoln's longtime opponent Stephen Douglas. Lincoln won the election with less than a majority of the popular vote and faced the prospect of leading a nation that was politically discontented and on the verge of civil war. Still not defeated in spirit after many discouraging and even debilitating blows, Lincoln left his home in Springfield, Illinois, on a cold and rainy day and stood tall as he gave a speech before going to the nation's capital. The President spoke above the sound of the pouring rain, a symbolic reminder of the bleak situation he faced:

> No one, not in my situation, can appreciate my feeling of sadness at this parting. . . . I now leave, not knowing when or whether ever I may return, with a task before me greater than that which rested upon [George] Washington. Without the assistance of that Divine Being who ever attended him, I cannot succeed. With that assistance I cannot fail. Trusting in Him who can go with me, and remain with you, and be everywhere for good, let us confidently hope that all will yet be well. To His care commending you, as I hope in your prayers you will commend me, I bid you an affectionate farewell.

Lincoln's belief in God was so linked to his own sense of

mission and worth that he proceeded on the basis of this faith. Not knowing what, how, or even when to do the things that needed to be done, he believed in his ability to accomplish the tasks before him because he knew that with "that assistance" he could not fail. Imagine the kind of faith and the sense of worth he must have had in order to go forward after so many defeats. Despite his gangly appearance and widespread unpopularity, he knew that God would give him the strength to succeed. This self-worth carried him through turbulent times and, to the surprise of many of his contemporaries, secured a place for him among America's greatest heroes.

What Does It Mean to Have Heavenly Parents?

Just as Lincoln maintained a sense of his unique mission by making a divine connection, we can discover our individual mission and fulfill it by letting Heavenly Father direct our lives. Faith in God and in His purposes is crucial to our discovery of self-worth. The truth that God is our Heavenly Parent and that He sees us as having unique reasons for being affirms (in the most meaningful way) that we have inherent value as individuals. In no greater way can we realize our self-worth and draw upon the power of this realization than by coming to know that God really is our Father.

As incomprehensible and wonderful as the creations of earth and space are, there is no creation as precious, even as sacred, as that of man and woman. "In the beginning God created the heaven and the earth. . . . And God saw every thing that he had made, and, behold, it was very good." (Genesis 1:1, 31.) But "God created man in his own image, in the image of God created he him; male and female created he them." (Genesis 1:27.) All of God's creations are pleasing to Him, but only we were created in His image. Could there be a more exalting and refining truth than that all of us are literally His children? Our lives can take on new meaning and purpose as we realize the certainty of our divine connection, of our likeness to Him.

Instead of wondering about the existence of God, look to the world around you and discover how it speaks of His glory. Instead of being fearful and frustrated—instead of doubting your own worth—remember that you are God's greatest creation. He knows and loves you. Just as the earth bespeaks God's majesty, the human mind, body, and spirit reflect His infinite love and—His Fatherly stewardship.

Sometimes it is easier to comprehend the eternal stewardship of our Heavenly Father—or our divine connection—by reflecting on the role of earthly stewards. Whether as a secretary, a supervisor, an inventor, an owner, or even a parent "creator" ourselves, we have all been stewards over someone or something. Even a little girl, dressed up as a clown at a family Halloween party, watched over her bag of hard-won candy with the all-seeing eye of real stewardship. She first spent several pensive moments lining up each delicacy and admiring its attractive packaging and unforgettable flavor. Later, when adults and other excited children approached her bag or even took a piece of her candy, she almost instinctively returned to check the contents. And every time, she knew exactly which piece was missing. Sometimes she would share with the new "owner" (relin-

quishing ownership), and other times she would demand
the candy's return. I was amazed by her careful stewardship.
She really seemed to know the status of all forty-seven pieces
of candy.

And somehow in the midst of this light-hearted observation, I caught a glimpse of how our Heavenly Father is
able to watch over and meet the needs of his billions of
children. In a small but meaningful way, the Savior's parable
of the lost sheep seemed to be acted out before my eyes:
"What man of you, having an hundred sheep, if he lose
one of them, doth not leave the ninety and nine in the
wilderness, and go after that which is lost, until he find it?
And when he hath found it, he layeth it on his shoulders,
rejoicing." (Luke 15:4–5.) This little three-year-old "shep-
herdess" knew when there was a lost "sheep" and faithfully
went to find it.

We see this same principle of stewardship at work whenever real caring, concern, compassion, or love accompanies
responsibility. I am acquainted with a former rancher who
says that he always knew when one of his cows was missing
from the pasture. He says that he could sense when there
were disputings in the herd, when illness rendered his cows
uncomfortable, and even when a cow seemed depressed in
spirit. Because this responsible rancher was so interested in
the welfare of each member of his herd, he detected their
individual needs and almost instinctively diagnosed any
problems.

In like fashion, good gardeners take interest in the lives
of their plants and flowers. When leaves are yellowing and
insects are invading, when the plants are crying out for

nourishment and strength, these caretakers come to the rescue with sprays, fertilizers, sunlight, and water. They know when a seed needs to be planted, when branches need to be pruned, when a transplant is necessary, and when the harvest is near.

Because they glory in the fruits of their labors, some gardeners even know their plants by name and care for each seedling in specialized ways. And when flowers are in full bloom and plants are yielding a bounteous harvest, they stop to enjoy the beauties before them.

While the stewardship of ranchers and gardeners reveals much about conscientious caretaking, the guardianship of good parents demonstrates our Heavenly Father's steward-ship as no other relationship can. I have marveled at my parents' ability to watch over seven children. They always seemed to know when one is hurting, experiencing quiet sorrow, struggling to understand, or even purporting silence when he or she really needs to talk.

The Creator and His Stewards

Once many years ago, even a stiff upper lip could not disguise my feelings of failure and disappointment from my sensitive parents. I had spent several months intensely pre-paring and carefully planning for an event of major im-portance and far-reaching implication. A lot of emotional, mental, and even physical energy had gone into the ac-complishment of this goal. And when my expectations were upset, when my efforts had been thwarted, I was deeply discouraged and even disheartened. But on the exterior, I acted as if nothing were wrong. I told my parents about the disappointment, but I made sure to let them know that "it didn't really matter." I offered them all of the proverbial explanations: "It was a good experience," "I sure learned a lot," and "There must have been a reason that it turned out this way." While these explanations were true, they were far from my real feelings at the time.

Somehow, my mother knew that I was more than mildly disappointed. She seemed to read my heart and mind and be aware of what I needed without my ever telling her. I came home from school the next day, and sitting on my bed was a small wooden plaque that read:

> Life's battles don't always go to the strongest or fastest; sooner or later, those who win are those who think they can.

I picked up the plaque and ran my fingers across the inscription. Tears began to form in the corners of my eyes as I realized how much my parents cared about me. They knew who I really was, and even when I temporarily lost sight of who I could become, they were there to remind me of my God-given potential. Because they had given me life, they helped me to have vision for that life.

Even now, when I look at that plaque—hanging on my office wall—I remember the quiet victory my parents helped me to achieve. That plaque, its message, and its unwritten sentiment have gone with me through several moves (and many more successes and disappointments), becoming more and more meaningful with life's experiences. Now, the plaque's message is not the only reason it is valuable to me, but the memories of the moment, the feelings of love and of being loved, make it a priceless treasure.

Just as our earthly parents participate in our personal creation (spiritually by molding our character, and physically by giving birth and sustaining our bodies), our Heavenly Father is the supreme Creator, shaping us and our lives by means of a perfect love. My parents, the rancher, the gardener, and even the little girl are all examples of earthly stewards who took care because they have love for their children, cows, plants — and even candies. They are (small "c") creators in their corner of the world, endeavoring to create pockets of love and concern wherever they may be. And so are we all creators: watching over and taking care of the people, places, and things for which we are lovingly responsible.

Imagine, then, the kind of care that our Heavenly Father takes as *the* Creator who unconditionally and universally loves. The Lord told His disciples that even a sparrow "shall not fall on the ground without your Father" knowing, and that "the very hairs of your head are all numbered" unto God. (Matthew 10:29–30.) This all-knowing and all-powerful Father is aware of the most intimate details of His children's lives. Not only does he know when our heads bow in humble prayer, but he even knows the very hairs that are on those heads.

I don't claim to fully understand such an omniscient and omnipotent stewardship. In many ways it is incomprehensible to me. But I do have faith in a loving Heavenly Father, and I am humbled by His personalized and perfect love for each of us.

One of a Kind

God truly is mindful of us as individuals. He knows us as unique sons and daughters with distinctive talents and different capabilities. And one of the greatest demonstrations of our inherent and infinite worth is the simple fact that no two human beings are exactly alike. Some may react cynically to that claim. I hear the doubtful moans and see the inquisitive glances every time I talk about what I call the "snowflake principle." (Even in the heaviest snowstorm, when inches upon inches of tiny snowflakes gather, no two snowflakes are exactly alike. When viewed under a microscope, each snowflake can be seen to be unique.) Every person over the eons of time is different from his or her fellow beings.

Robert Fulghum looks into the statistics behind this uniqueness in his best-selling book *All I Really Need to Know I Learned in Kindergarten:*

> The statisticians figure that about 60 billion people have been born so far. And . . . there's no telling how many more there will be, but it looks like a lot. And yet — and here comes the statistic of statistics — with all the possibilities for variation among the sex cells produced by each person's parents, it seems quite certain that each one of the billions of human beings who has ever existed has been distinctly different from every other human being, and that this will continue for the indefinite future.
>
> In other words, if you were to line up on one side of the earth every human being who ever lived or ever will live, and you took a good look at the whole motley crowd, *you wouldn't find anybody quite like you.*[2]

What more empowering and motivating thought could there be than this knowledge that *you are the only you*. Our Heavenly Father knows us so intimately and so completely that, even if we are a twin and look like someone else, He created a distinctly different person in each of us. (Even identical twins have different fingerprints.) And because He knows us so individually and loves us so unconditionally, we really can accomplish any worthy goal with His Fatherly providence.

I once shared the "snowflake principle" with a rambunctious group of middle-school students. There were more than five hundred children in a small auditorium. Half of them were sitting on the floor, and all of them were anxiously whispering and eagerly watching the clock during the last hour of the day. I was the lucky "entertainer" of this less-than-interested crowd.

They probably did not hear much else of what I said that hour, but I will long remember their attentive faces when I told them that they were unique individuals, completely different from every other human being. Even though, in the hour we spent together, thousands of people would be born and thousands more would die, there was no one in that room who was the same as anyone else who had ever lived. For a brief moment, bodies stopped wiggling, mouths stopped whispering, heads turned, and eyes filled with childlike wonderment. For only a second, they seemed to catch a vision of their one-of-a-kind worth. Somehow, these distracted middle schoolers were grabbed by the thought that no one else was quite like them. No longer were they just another student (all with the same haircut, same brand of jeans, and same type of folder), but in their minds' eyes—if only momentarily—they saw the unique individuals who they are. They caught a glimpse of their self-worth.

Unlimited and Amazing Worth

For many years, scientists underestimated the worth (from a strictly chemical standpoint) of the human body itself. Professors used to say that the chemical composition of a human being was worth about thirty-two dollars on the going market. But as the late Earl Nightingale (the well-known self-improvement author) pointed out, since the age of atomic chemistry, scientists now calculate that if the electronic energy in the hydrogen atoms of the body could be used, each human being could supply the electricity for a large, highly industrialized country for nearly one week! As one duPont scientist determined: "The average person—by this estimate—is worth about 85 billion dollars!" Certainly, any human being is worth even more than that dollar amount, but this estimation—or rather underestimation—of worth is indicative of the shortsightedness to which many of us subject ourselves. Whether it be a monetary label for actual physical worth or the subconscious label we give to ourselves, one of the most damaging devices to our personal progress is the failure to believe in our own worth—or in the worth of others.

If we think we are only a "thirty-two-dollar" person and others are only "thirty-two dollar" people, only "thirty-two-dollar" goals will be accomplished, and only "thirty-two-dollar" expectations will be met. But when we realize that

God sees us for our "eighty-five-billion-dollar-plus" capabilities and attributes, we capitalize on our unique strengths in such a way that they reflect our infinite worth. If we belittle ourselves, His creations, it is easy to criticize the Creator — which can lead to loss of faith and spiritual alienation.

We Walk by Faith

Without question, such a belief in ourselves and in our infinite capacities may require a courageous leap of faith. Ultimately, we do all that we are capable of doing and become all that we were meant to become when we turn to God for personal vision. It could not be more clear than in the gospel according to Luke: "With God nothing shall be impossible." (Luke 1:37.)

Jesus also said, "If ye have faith . . . nothing shall be impossible unto you," and "all things are possible to him that believeth." (Matthew 17:20; Mark 9:23.) When we believe these words and exercise our faith in Him, spiritual growth becomes possible.

Of course, such change is still not necessarily easy. And our natural tendency is to continue in the way we were, staying in our familiar paths, focusing on things that really may not matter much. But faith in our Heavenly Father helps us to move into new and sometimes uncomfortable territory — in other words, to grow.

Faith also carries us through the things in life that seem beyond our present understanding — through pain, sorrow, and disappointment. We may feel worried about what tomorrow will bring. But for today, we can find comfort in the fact that our Father knows us and loves us, and that in the end He will wipe all the tears from our eyes.

We do not know all the answers. But we can rest assured that God does, and that we can put our trust in Him. As Victor Hugo wrote: "Have courage for the great sorrows of life, and patience for the small ones; and when you have laboriously accomplished your daily task, go to sleep in peace. God is awake."

All things are possible when we believe enough to make a personal leap, when we trust enough to turn our lives over to God.

The Leap of Faith

A leap of faith is exactly what a young American pilot made during the air campaign in World War II. Enemy Japanese fire shot his plane down in the middle of deep Pacific waters. The startled pilot struggled to free himself from his aircraft, only to discover that both Japanese and U.S. ships were racing to his "rescue." Uncertain as to whether he would be saved or imprisoned, the pilot prayed for help and believed in his ability to hang on. To this day, President George Bush asserts that it was more than luck that brought the American submarine to his aid just moments before the Japanese vessel. Friends of Mr. Bush say that he firmly believes that God spared his life for a reason. And as a conversation with a friend during the 1991 Persian Gulf War reveals, he still derives personal strength and inspiration from this belief in God. President Bush explained: "Now I can really understand Lincoln. This is a place [the White House] that makes you want to pray."[3]

We may have never jumped from an aircraft, but each of us does our own sort of "leaping" when we make decisions based upon faith. Sometimes when we turn our restricted sight over to God's omniscient seeing, we have to make a pretty substantial jump (whether mental, emotional, spiritual, or even physical) from where we have been to where we know, with God, we can go.

One such jump in my life was when I left my job in Pennsylvania and returned to Utah. I had been working as a TV news anchor for a CBS affiliate station in Pennsylvania for several years. I enjoyed my work and was doing well at it. But when it came time to renew my contract, my thoughts turned homeward to a recently widowed mother, family, and other (at-the-time-unknown) reasons to return to Utah. I was not completely sure why I was choosing to go home. I just felt like it was the right thing for me to do—even though it did not seem like a smart career move.

The general manager at the TV station called me into his office many times, rating sheets in his hands, trying to persuade me to stay—and trying to figure out why I would go. He wondered if another station had given me a better offer and was willing to present counteroffers to get me to stay. He kept questioning, "Is it money? Do you need more money? Let's decide on a better salary." In his mind, money was the only logical reason to quit, and the personal explanations I gave for leaving had to be "excuses" for receiving a better salary offer somewhere else. But I was returning to Utah without a job—or even any real prospects for employment.

When I got to Utah, the jobs were not waiting, but they were to be found. And with the perspective of many years, I look back on the blessings and opportunities that

have come since my return to Utah and recognize God's
hand in directing my life. He knew better than I what my
talents were and how they could best be used. I made a
leap, and He certainly caught me with the open arms and
reassuring embraces of bounteous blessings and inspiring
opportunities. I, like the poet, took the road less traveled
by, and that *has* made all the difference.

You have probably done the same thing: made a courageous leap of faith and then reflected on how it has "made
all the difference" in your life. People come to such cross-
roads thousands of times a day in a million different places,
and they similarly make decisions without knowing the
"why" but believing in the "how." Something as simple as
taking an alternate route to work — for no apparent reason —
may change the course of our day's events; listening to a
different radio station may put us in touch with just the
"right" song or message; signing up for another class may
give us the very information, and even encouragement, we
were secretly searching for; and sending an unexpected
"hello" might make all the difference in the life of someone
dear to us. We need only look to the Wellspring of all
"hows," believe in ourselves to accomplish the "whens,"
and wait to uncover the divinely inspired "whys."

The Gift of Creation

God, as our Heavenly Father and the Perfect Steward,
is ready and waiting to guide us, as believers. When we
trust Him enough to hear the quiet whisperings of our own
hearts and minds (to believe in the dreams and aspirations
that are uniquely ours), we begin to realize the unlimited

possibilities that are ours to behold. We believe to see, and we no longer need to see that we might believe.

As creators ourselves, we emulate the Creator of all things, exercising a divinely inspired stewardship. Even while we are engaged in our own earthly molding, we become clay in His hands. Our faith makes us whole. (See Matthew 9:22.) We become better and accomplish more than we thought possible when we realize that seeing always falls short of inspired believing—and that, with God, achieving the "impossible" (the difficult and the challenging) is our birthright. In order to realize our worth, we walk by faith, and other times even make leaps of faith. Our Heavenly Father will be there to guide us—and at times even carry us—along life's customized path as we live up to the greatness within us. And even though the road is oftentimes long and many times hard, realizing our self-worth will help us to weather the storms and walk through the rough places. Believing that God knows us as individuals, with unique talents and distinctive purposes, is a necessary step to making lasting change and experiencing a real transformation.

CHAPTER 5

ETERNAL PRECEPTS, NOT TEMPORARY TACTICS

Nothing comes from nothing. Nothing ever could.
— Richard Rodgers

Unlike the quick-fix (and subsequently short-lived) tactics that have characterized our society in recent years, the process of realizing our self-worth takes time. And while quick-fix strategies promise timely results, the recognition of self-worth incites a timeless transformation. But in a world where fast-pace is often the only pace, it is sometimes hard to see beyond the whirling starts and cosmetic stops of temporary improvement. The more steady and sometimes even staggering steps of real, inside-out improvement are largely less dramatic — and sometimes even invisible.

Our lives may be so inundated by quick-fix improvements that we may not even recognize them as such. Only when we take a few moments to get out of the pool of temporary self-help tactics will we be able to discern some of the superficial strokes and artificial buoys of "immediate" self-improvement. Our homes, offices, literature, media, and mailboxes are full of such quick-and-easy remedies. Sweepstakes, lotteries, and gambling "get-aways" solicit our subscriptions and beg for our "donations" (and charge-card numbers!). In return, their million-dollar prizes promise a life of extravagance and leisure. All we have to do is scrape the silver lining, "sign here," attach the lucky sticker, or return the winning number—and wealth untold will be showered upon us. We want to believe that this *is* our lucky break, that we will never have to work another day, that we will be driving away in that new sports car, "living the good life" in a luxurious new home—that we really can get something for nothing.

The Quick-and-Easy Way

This quick-fix mentality does not stop with promises of wealth and possessions. Life-changing guarantees are made about our very character, personality, habits, and even our body. If we subscribe to a certain magazine, repeat a designated phrase, go to a particular school, or even listen to a subliminal tape, all of our problems will be solved. We will be instantly changed into the kind of person we have always dreamed of becoming.

This advertisement I received in the mail exemplifies such an "overnight" mentality:

> Instant Personal Charm
> Want to succeed in life and draw others to you? Order our tapes now. Simply play these subliminal tapes at night, while you sleep, and you will find new power in your relationships. You will unleash the natural charm and magnetism within you. You'll stop self-defeating behaviors and draw on the power of the subconscious. You'll automatically take on the actions of a charismatic individual—so that others will want to be around you and want to cooperate with you. Only $19.99. Order now!

By simply playing a tape or flipping a switch, we change into the charismatic, magnetic individual we have long dreamed of becoming!

Most bookstores — and scores of mail-order companies — sell books and tapes that pledge a "perfect" body. After just reading this book or thirty days of regularly listening to this tape, slim thighs and a flat stomach are the easily achieved by-products. Success stories and pictures of beautifully shaped, gorgeous people decorate the books' and tapes' covers, while exercise, a balanced diet, discipline, and all the other things we so painfully associate with weight control may be replaced by a collection of pills and positive thoughts. We all know (perhaps too well) that there is more to losing weight than simply hearing positive thoughts. If listening to a tape were all that was necessary to have a trim body, obesity would have been "cured" long ago.

Just like the promises made by the snake-oil salesmen of the Old West, these companies claim to have discovered the eternal elixir, the fountain of youth, the missing link to personal empowerment. And many of us fall prey to their pledges. We want to be able to buy success, plug in happiness, put on a perfect body, and tap into a guru who has all the answers. As Bednar and Peterson describe in *Spirituality and Self-Esteem:* "Most of us like things the quick and easy way. You know, a pill for pain and cash for class. We live in a world where appearances seem more important than reality, and the difference between appearance and reality is not as clear as it once was."[1] We want to alter reality so that it will conform to the easily acquired appearance of success that has been defined for us by so many external sources.

Consider, for example, the late-night television sales programs that are set in what seems to be a newsroom. The would-be anchor sits behind a desk and describes the latest product from his authoritative position as the bearer of good news. The marketing technique is manipulative and even deceptive. We hear about an amazing device (*once-in-a-lifetime opportunity!*) that miraculously cures pain, an innovative program (*with proven results!*) for getting rich in our spare time, and even a plan for becoming effortlessly wealthy through real estate (*no money down!*). Realizing that consumers largely look to the news for facts and information, the companies present their products as if they were newsworthy breakthroughs. They make their ads into "reports" and present their products as if they were life-changing advances in science and technology.

On another channel, at about the same sleepless hour, we are told to dial a toll-free number for psychic readings. If we just press a few buttons and give a little background information, our whole life will pass before our ears and eyes. No more guessing and wondering.

The appeal may be to a family, a corporation, or even to an individual, but the promise for a quick fix is all the same. Whether on TV, in a magazine, over the telephone, or in the mail, we hear about amazing seminars that will immediately change an organization's deep-seated financial, cultural, managerial, and other problems. Many high-level executives invite seminar speakers to talk — for an hour and maybe even for a day — to change the corporate culture, the employees' work habits, or the managerial mindset. They want to buy an easy, painless solution to all their corporate ills. Or at least, they want some literature that will answer all of their questions and solve all of their problems. While speakers and books can present them with some of the tools to make significant changes, their corporations will not be changed overnight. And any medium that promises such an instant turnaround is suspect of using temporary repair tactics, not timeless transformation techniques. If managers expect an immediate, all-inclusive, *and* lasting cure, they may be disappointed in a week or so when the Band-Aids come off and the sores are still there.

This is not to say that many popular self-improvement strategies cannot be beneficial and even helpful. The long road to change includes many smaller paths of progress — paths that are defined by learned and practiced directives. For example, regulating our diet according to the latest weight reduction program is better — usually — than not monitoring our diet at all. Just as balancing our time according to the most fashionable time-management program is one step closer to efficiency than keeping no schedule whatsoever. But behind the skills and strategies we will discuss in this book is the primary — and abiding — belief that we are children of God who have the capacity, and even the responsibility to take good care of our physical bodies and to use our time productively. When our divine connection motivates our efforts, the improvement process becomes more steady, meaningful, and even transforming.

Personality Ethic versus Character Ethic

In *Seven Habits of Highly Effective People,* Stephen R. Covey labels the quick-fix, superficial-solution mentality as the "Personality Ethic" and juxtaposes it with an internally based, principle-centered approach to life that he calls the "Character Ethic." His research into the first 200 years of American success literature shows that (roughly) the first 150 years of self-improvement theory were founded on "basic principles of effective living": things like integrity, humility, fidelity, justice, patience, industry, and the Golden Rule. However, the success literature of the next 50 years of American history "became more a function of personality, of public image, of attitudes and behaviors, skills and techniques, that lubricate the processes of human interaction." He summarizes: "Reference to the Character Ethic became mostly lip service; the basic thrust was quick-fix influence techniques, power strategies, communication skills, and positive attitudes."[2]

The reasons for self-improvement evolved from inner, God-fearing transformation to outward, peer-approving pacification, and the methods for changing became more appearance and "success" oriented than principle-centered. The trend was not just to be involved in a program for personal progress but to improve *quickly* — and to be successful *now.*

"Be Ye Transformed"

All of this sharply contrasts with the Lord's plan for lasting progression. The scriptures tell us, "Precept must be upon precept . . . line upon line; here a little, and there a little." (Isaiah 28:10.) Real self-improvement is not going to take place all at once. Just as a poor self-esteem will not be changed with a single instance of praise or a moment of self-congratulation, our self-worth will not be discovered overnight. The eternal evolution of our character begins one precept at a time. And no matter how many times we try to be a better communicator, a more efficient worker, or a more loving spouse, our efforts will fall short if they are not based on eternal precepts, foremost of which is the awareness that we are truly children of God. Without understanding the value God places on a person's life, popular self-improvements would be superficial sutures for a wounded self-esteem. If we try to find self-worth in money, jobs, possessions, or personal relationships, what happens when those things fade or fail? If our God-given worth is not the motivating force behind all change, we will not experience real and everlasting change. We will not be transformed through Christ. As Paul admonished in his epistle to the Romans: "Be not conformed to this world: but *be ye transformed by the renewing of your mind,* that ye may prove what is that good, and acceptable, and perfect, will of God." (Romans 12:2; italics added.) We renew our minds by seeking after all that is good, acceptable, perfect, or of God. And by so doing, we are not just changed, altered, or adjusted, but we are *transformed.*

When our thoughts and actions are *not* "conformed to this world," when we are *not* set on making instant progress and measuring success by visible, worldly standards, we will be transformed into the noble sons and daughters our Heavenly Father sees us as becoming. But how do we "renew our minds" and fully understand our self-worth? How can we experience such a transformation? By first understanding that the choices we make, the actions we take, and the thoughts we entertain will bring us closer to or farther away from such a life-changing recognition.

In other words, taking responsibility for the things we say and do is prerequisite to real change. This vital correspondence between making conscionable choices and deeply understanding our inherent worth is the missing link in most self-improvement programs. We cannot expect to improve in any lasting way or to fully comprehend our divine connection if we are making wrong choices, thinking bad thoughts, engaging in unwholesome activities, and wasting our time. But when we are making right choices, thinking good thoughts, engaging in wholesome activities, and productively using our time and energies, the resultant blessing is one of knowing who we really are.

While we do not have to do anything to get self-worth (it is an inherent, free gift from God), we must make daily efforts to remember this worth. And perhaps the best way to explain how to recognize our self-worth is by first exploring how *not* to merit such a recognition. If we make choices that separate us from God and that lead us to discount our own worthiness, how can we then expect to look to God for an appreciation of our worth? Our Heavenly Father will never withdraw this infinite and unchanging gift of worth from us, but we may withdraw ourselves from Him — and from a recognition of our worth — by doing things that make us feel less than worthy. When we are discouraged by guilt, overwhelmed by busy preoccupation, or hardened

by wrongdoing, our burdened spirits may not give way to
such a lofty truth.

Abraham Lincoln explained the other side of this truth:
"It is difficult to make a man miserable while he feels he is
worthy of himself and claims kindred to the great God who
made him." When we are making even small strides to feel
better about ourselves and the kind of life we are living,
we are in a more conducive position to discover our worth.
Exercising, eating right, learning, reading, and engaging in
the kinds of self-improvements that we all know about are
the "leafy branches of the tree," the outward manifestations
that lead to real growth and change. But the deep roots
that give all change stability and strength are sustained by
a vital understanding of our self-worth. We make a godly
change, or transformation by digging deep inside ourselves,
earnestly praying, and seeking the Lord's help in acquiring
a harvest of meaningful improvements.

Three A's of Change

The three A's of change are a convenient way to explain
and to remember the precepts of godly transformation:

1. Awareness.
2. Acceptance.
3. Action.

An *awareness* of our individual worth is essential to the
transformation process. We must search to know truth, to
raise our level of consciousness, and to become more sensitive to whether we are moving toward—or away from—
a greater understanding of our self-worth. I believe that

most of us, whether in the deepest recesses of our minds or the center of our hearts, believe in God. As the Psalmist wrote thousands of years ago: "The fool hath said in his heart, There is no God." (Psalm 14:1.) And as Ralph Waldo Emerson wrote in our own dispensation, "All I have seen teaches me to trust the creator for all that I have not seen." No matter what our religious background and beliefs may be, most people innately sense the need for a Divine Being.

With that belief in place, an awareness that we are His children does not require much stretching. Because there is a God in heaven, it would only make sense that He is our Heavenly Father and that we are His children. This initial and empowering awareness that God is our Father sets a pattern for every ensuing opportunity for change. Before we decide to improve some specific thing about ourselves or our situation, we must first be aware of the need for change.

As we discussed earlier, our values and feelings of self-worth — while ever present — need to be brought to a higher level of consciousness if they are to be deeply understood. For example, if we have a million dollars in the bank, it does us no good if we don't know the money is there. How can we make use of a million dollars without ever realizing it is in our possession? Do you realize that you are breathing right now? Did you know you just blinked your eyes? Probably not. Or at least you were probably not thinking about these involuntary processes — even while you were engaging in them. But these rhetorical questions did raise your level of consciousness. In the same way that breathing and blinking subconsciously help maintain our physical bodies, our values or beliefs—whether we recognize them as such or not—govern our mental, emotional, and even spiritual processes. And if these values are to reflect an awareness of our self-worth, we must first be cognizant of what they are right now and then take note of either their congruence or disparity with our self-worth. We must stop to observe how aware we are of the eternal truth that God is our Heavenly Father. As Jeremiah outlined: "Ye shall seek me, and find me, when ye shall search for me with all your heart." (Jeremiah 29:13.) We must pause to evaluate our mental "breathing" and spiritual "blinking" before we know to breathe harder or softer, blink sooner or later. We must search with all our heart to become *aware* of our personal relationship with God.

An *acceptance* of that awareness is another step on the long road to change. We addressed the idea of acceptance in somewhat different terms (but with the same end in mind) when we talked about faith in chapter 4. A vital step in becoming empowered by our self-worth is simply believing, or having faith, in God and knowing that He is our Heavenly Father. When we really accept our God-given inheritance, we make a significant (and necessary) step toward realizing our self-worth.

We cannot make claim to our divine inheritance if we don't first believe that it really has been given to us. As Paul advised Timothy (and all of us): "*Neglect not the gift that is in thee. . . .* Meditate upon these things; give thyself wholly to them; that thy profiting may appear to all. Take heed unto thyself, and unto the doctrine; continue in them: for in doing this thou shalt both save thyself, and them that hear thee." (1 Timothy 4:14–16; italics added.) This acceptance of "the gift that is in thee" leads to all other meaningful changes. We then accept responsibility for our actions — whether good or ill — and realize that the future is ours, and only ours, to mold. By embracing our divine endowment of worth, we accept responsibility for whatever changes we make. Life becomes a do-it-yourself-with-God project.

And finally, after we are aware of our self-worth and internalize that awareness, we are in a position to take *action* — to really make change. When we believe that God is a loving Heavenly Father who knows each of us as individuals, we can accomplish all worthy goals. By becoming aware of and accepting our God-given worth, we align our beliefs with this empowering truth — and really become free: free to do the possible and the impossible, with God. Jesus bore testimony of the power that comes from turning to God to take meaningful action: "All things, whatsoever ye shall ask in prayer, believing, ye shall receive." (Matthew 21:22.) Action that is incited by humble prayer will not only bring desired results but will also be aligned with our unique potential.

Perhaps the most important catalyst of change is the sincere prayer of the humble believer. No greater testimony is born of our inherent worth than the peaceful assurance that comes from asking God, in a moment of private petitioning, on bended knee, if He knows us personally and if He loves us unconditionally as His children.

I believe that God hears and answers our prayers and will bless us with the comforting assurance that *He knows and loves us.* Such prayer may not only give us the strength to take *action*, but it may also give us an *awareness* — and the ability to *accept* the awareness — that we are children of God. In other words, while I presented the three A's of change as if they were consecutive components of improvement (each building on the last), in reality they are more likely to occur concurrently than sequentially.

Sometimes we may take *action* first, and then, because of the good feeling that results, become *aware* of our divine endowment of worth and begin to believe in — or *accept* — our infinite capabilities. Other times, we may faithfully *accept* a principle of godly improvement, and, from that acceptance, become inspired to raise our level of *awareness* and then take *action*.

As is the case with all truth, these components of change are circumscribed into a synergistic whole, powerfully feeding into each other. Graphically, this cycle of growth looks something like the diagram on the next page, concentrically building.

Reality Hits

But common sense is not always common practice. Most of us know doctors who smoke, accountants who don't balance their checkbooks, and management consultants who mismanage their own employees. Undoubtedly, all of us have knowledge we fail to take advantage of. It's not *what* we know that really matters but what we *do* with what we know. We may "talk the talk" but never "walk the walk."

No matter how well we may memorize the three A's

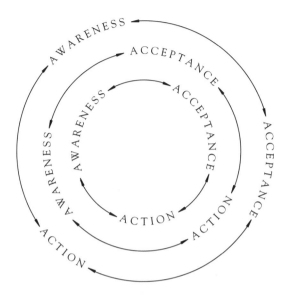

and talk about their importance, if our actions do not begin to incorporate their essence, we might just as well not know them. And perhaps more primary, if our actions do not begin to be inspired by the knowledge of our self-worth, we deprive ourselves of the life-changing power that comes from this recognition.

Have you ever been excited about a new self-improvement program? Maybe you go to a seminar, read a book, or listen to a tape that gets you all fired up to be a better person. So you decide to awake the next morning at the crack of dawn, jog a mile, eat a balanced breakfast, and do some inspirational reading—all before you go to work.

But when the alarm goes off, *reality hits*. Suddenly five o'clock seems like an unearthly hour, the early morning temperature is much colder than you remembered, and the inspirational "rah-rah" never seemed so lifeless. So you hit the snooze button and vow that *tomorrow* you'll start your superhuman self-improvement program.

We pacify ourselves with the illusion that it will be easier to begin *tomorrow*. Sometimes we fool ourselves by thinking that we will change overnight, that we will be as different as the night is from the day—*tomorrow*. Peter De Vries has written a one-liner that explains this sentiment well: "Sooner or later reality trundles each of us into surgery for an illusionectomy." Let's hope it's just a minor outpatient operation and not a major hospital-stay surgery.

Dramatize the Commitment

We all set unrealistic goals from time to time. One way of bridging this gap between wishful thinking and realistic action is by dramatizing the commitment to act. In other words, if we know that as children of God we should take care of the physical bodies He has given us (part of the stewardship with which He has entrusted us), we not only recognize the need for exercise, but, *as stewards*, we also realize our ability to exercise.

Somewhere between knowing we need to exercise and actually beginning to do it, we can easily lose interest. But when we dramatize our commitment by doing some specific thing to get us excited, we give ourselves additional impetus to take the first step. If we buy a new pair of jogging shoes, map out an alternate exercise route, or give our bike a thorough cleaning and lubrication, we make our personal commitment more visible to ourselves. We envision the end that we want to achieve—and make firm our commitment to achieve it—when we go out of our way to act out that commitment.

Share the Information

Another helpful forerunner in taking action (and for internalizing the ideas in this book) is sharing the knowledge we have acquired or the commitments we have made with others. Immediately after information has been presented to us, most of us remember only 50 percent of what we learned. Within a couple of days, we remember even less. After one week, we usually remember only a small percentage of what we initially learned.[3] But when we share that information with someone else (either right after we learned it or shortly thereafter), we invariably remember much more of the information.

The best way to learn something is to become a teacher, to share what we have learned with loved ones, family, co-workers, friends, or neighbors. The simple act of shifting from learner to teacher significantly facilitates our learning, and our acting upon those precepts and practices we have been taught. The same principle applies in setting a goal. If we share our commitment with someone else, if we even write our commitment down or voice that commitment in private prayer, we are much more likely to achieve that goal.

Walk Before We Run

Another important precept for enacting real change is to master simple tasks before complex ones. A major goal of far-reaching effect is not achieved in a day—or maybe even in a year, many years, or a lifetime. Comedian Eddie Cantor was quick to observe that it took him "twenty years to become an overnight sensation"!

You have probably proven this principle true in your own life. Have you ever rushed out the door, grabbing whatever edible objects were in sight, rationalizing to yourself that at least you were eating "breakfast." You feel fine for the first two hours of the day, but about mid-morning, all the energy you ever had seems to drain from your body. And you just can't quite "get it together" the rest of the day.

Or have you ever gotten up fifteen minutes early, eaten a full breakfast, and maybe even taken a moment or two to organize your thoughts, read something uplifting, and pray? The rest of the day seems to go smoother, you have more energy than usual, and you seem to get twice as much done. It is a simple task, but it has far-reaching effects. (Notice I called them simple — not easy — tasks. Not all simple tasks are easy, but many are worthwhile.) Eating a good breakfast puts us in a better position to solve more complex problems throughout the day. We cannot expect to have a balanced-breakfast day (or life) if we only take time for an instant-breakfast beginning to that day (and life).

In the same way, we cannot expect to run a marathon if all we have ever run is the 100-yard dash. If we are out of shape and suddenly become enthusiastic about exercising, we may be disappointed when we can't run ten miles on the first day. There are no shortcuts to real fitness.

Even spiritual aerobics are difficult if we begin with the

"high-intensity" workout. But if we remember that we get in shape (physically, mentally, and spiritually) by taking one step at a time, reading one line upon another, learning one precept after the next, our growth will be much more fulfilling and life-changing. As the classical thinker Publilius said, "It takes a long time to bring excellence to maturity." And it does. But the journey toward fully realizing our self-worth becomes as worthwhile as the actual destination when we maintain a godly vision for our lives — and proceed with genuine effort.

As with all meaningful change, personal battles must be waged before public victories can be expected. "Intra" (or inner) development must precede "inter" (or outer) influence. We must be working on our own challenges before we can help with others' problems. We must become our own caretaker before we can become a caregiver. We must make deposits in our own account before we can make withdrawals — for ourselves and for others.

The Journey of Self-Improvement

Self-worth may not be in the dictionary, but it will be the focal point of our journey as we make the divine connection to self-improvement. When we picture our life through the visionary viewfinder of inherent worth, we capture a world of untapped possibilities and a self of infinite capabilities. The developmental process itself becomes a sacred proving ground as we look to God to process clearly focused pictures of authentic success — and not Instamatic snapshots of what only seems to be success.

Regardless of where we have been, where we are going

right now is what matters. And we can remember the words of Richard L. Evans:

> Life moves in one direction only—and each day we are faced with an actual set of circumstances, not with what might have been, not with what we might have done, but with what is, and with where we are now—and from this point we must proceed: not from where we were, not from where we wish we were—but from where we are.[4]

Now is the time to set out on a self-improvement journey that will take us where we have always wanted to be: to our best selves in an even better world. The discovery of our self-worth is an exciting and empowering journey. As T. S. Eliot has written:

> We must not cease from exploration, and the end of all our exploring will be to arrive where we began and to know the place for the first time.

Frequently, what may at first seem new and unique is simply the excitement of discovering something very old— something that we've just begun to see or understand for ourselves. When Columbus discovered America, the continent had existed for millennia, but it was new to this band of explorers—so new they didn't at first recognize it as "the new world." Columbus didn't *invent* America—he discovered it. Likewise Newton didn't *invent* gravity—he described it. Edison didn't *invent* electricity—he discovered how to tap it.

We all make new discoveries when, for the first time, we understand and comprehend *who we really are*, who we always have been, and who we always will be: children of God. We will experience a quiet explosion of the eternal potential God has given to each of us as we make the divine connection. We will discover the power that is already within us but that, for many of us, may be realized "for the first time."

SECTION 3

. . . .

TURNING INWARD

We *can* change and improve.
A real understanding of our self-worth
empowers us to reach our God-given potential.

CHAPTER 6

BEYOND SELF-TALK AND VISUALIZATION

Certain thoughts are prayers. There are moments when, whatever the attitude of the body, the soul is on its knees.
— Victor Hugo

Positive thinking, self-talk, and visualization are primary components of self-improvement literature. And justifiably so. These practices are sound, and they have proven to be positive and powerful influences in the lives of many. The Proverbs taught thousands of years ago that "as he thinketh in his heart, so is he" and "a merry heart maketh a cheerful countenance." (Proverbs 23:7; 15:13.) In other words, how we talk to ourselves and what we think about ourselves contribute to who we will become and how we will feel about ourselves. But real, transforming self-improvement is more than just thinking and talking positively.

When we recognize and respect our eternal worth, we do more than change the way we talk to ourselves and the way we see ourselves. Our very thought processes and patterns of behavior come to reflect our divine nature. Positive self-talk becomes an empowering form of personal prayer; and hopeful visualization evolves into purposeful foresight.

Taking the "Self" out of Self-Talk

Whether we are aware of it or not, every hour of every day we have an ongoing conversation with ourselves. An inner voice talks to us all day — and all night — long. (If you don't believe it, it's the voice that just asked, "What voice?") In the musical *Fiddler on the Roof,* the Jewish father Tevye regularly engages in such conversation with himself — and with his God. He is so accustomed to verbalizing his thoughts and addressing them to God that, at one point, he even tells God what the "Good Book" says. He quickly chuckles at the thought that he is telling God what is in the Bible, but this "slip" artfully demonstrates how self-talk can become "prayer-talk" when, like Tevye, we include our Heavenly Father in our everyday introspections. If Tevye is confronted with a problem or forced to make a decision, he takes a minute to reason with himself and then to present his reasoning to God. When his daughter asks permission to marry outside the Jewish faith, he goes back and forth with himself — and with God. "On the one hand," he says, and "on the other hand," he continues, until he eventually grants his daughter permission to marry the man she loves. For Tevye, and for each of us, the most important conversations we have are the ones we have with ourselves and with God.

When our self-talk is inspired by the knowledge that we really are children of God, we not only change the nature of our conversations, but we also have more to talk about. Our personal musings become heartfelt prayers, and our inner voice speaks silent praises to God. Emerson so aptly explains in "Self-Reliance": "Prayer is the contemplation of the facts of life from the highest point of view."

Or, the contemplation of the facts of life from the highest point of view *is* prayer. Our self-talk becomes prayer when we consider ourselves and our surroundings from that lofty viewpoint. When we realize our inherent worth, our inner monologue becomes an inspiring dialogue with God. We take the "self" out of self-talk and participate in real communion (or a two-way interchange of feelings, thoughts, and ideas) and not just self-centered exposition.

Unfortunately, research indicates that some 75 percent of our self-talk is negative [1]—let alone divinely connected. Our alarm goes off in the morning, and we tell ourselves that it is going to be a terrible day. We look in the mirror and wonder why we look so awful. We miss our bus and reprimand ourselves for being late. We sometimes go through a whole day saying rude and damaging things to ourselves—things that we would probably not even say to other people. Do any of these exclamations sound familiar: "I can't believe how stupid I am!" "Why did I even get out of bed today!" "With my luck, I'll probably fail anyway." "Who could ever love me?"

Playing the Inner Game First

I have engaged in this sort of negative mental programming while golfing. On several occasions, I have teed off with all the force and energy I have ever put into a swing—only to watch my ball roll off the tee and land just a few feet from where I was standing. I would say things to myself like: "This is going to be a bad day," "I can tell I am just not up to par today." Or on times when I have lost several balls to an embarrassingly avoidable pond, I caught myself saying: "You blew it, Lloyd." "Those were some lousy shots." "You've lost your touch." I would have never said such degrading things to my family and friends, but somehow it was all right for *me* to chastise myself. And when I complained about hitting a ball in the high grass, in what is called "the rough," I let the same negative thoughts govern my performance.

In *The Power of Positive Thinking,* Norman Vincent Peale asserts that "the rough" in golf—and in the game of life— is primarily mental. He tells his own golfing story of how he hit a ball in the rough only to receive some of his own advice from his golfing partner. His partner reminded him to think positively: "All you need to do is to keep your eye on that ball and tell yourself that you are going to lift it out of that grass with a lovely stroke." Dr. Peale thanked his partner for the positive reinforcement, and, as would be expected, proceeded to hit the ball back onto the fairway. From that experience, he makes the following assertion: "Believe that Almighty God has put in you the power to lift yourself out of the rough by keeping your eyes firmly fixed on the source of your power. Affirm to yourself that through this power you can do anything you have to do. . . . Believe this, and a sense of victory will come."[2]

In Dr. Peale's own words, the key to his successful stroke was not in the positive programming alone but, more important, in his recognition that "Almighty God put in [him] the power to lift [himself] out of the rough." The recognition of this inherent power—or divinely endowed worth—was the greater enabler. The positive programming was only the rightful reflection and the necessary forerunner of this more illuminating belief. The rough was not so rough because, more than just thinking positive thoughts, Dr. Peale believed in his God-given power to "do anything [he had] to do."

This empowering sort of positive self-talk is not selfish aggrandizement. My negative conversation with myself while golfing, however, *was* subtly selfish. I was worried about how *I* looked: about *my* form, *my* golf balls, and *my* score. My degrading monologue was more self-centered than any of the "I-can-do-anything" thoughts that Dr. Peale summarized — because (even in simple things like a game of golf) his source of strength was a belief in God.

And while the positive thoughts of Dr. Peale's golfing companion were superficially unselfish, this kind of self-talk is more in line with the popular understanding of positive self-talk: sow positive thoughts and we will reap positive results. This mode of thinking is not to be minimalized. There is certainly a place for such a belief in ourselves and in our mind's capacity to turn belief into achievement. But whether Dr. Peale realized it or not, he took his companion's remarks one step further and said, in effect, that we should be positive and expect positive results *because* we are children of God, the beneficiaries of a divine inheritance of power. In other words, by believing in himself *and* in his God, he prayed himself into a successful stroke — and into a more fulfilling life. He did more than just think his own positive thoughts; he drew upon the strength of God and turned self-talk into prayer-talk.

When we approach the "rough" in life with a positive attitude *and* a humble dependence upon God, it is amazing how the rocky road we were once traveling can become so much more smooth. The nature of "the road" really does not change, but our capacity to walk it increases when we turn to God for support. We, like Paul, will then say to ourselves: "I can do all things *through Christ which strengtheneth me.*" (Philippians 4:13; italics added.) Even the "can-do" self-talk of a positive thinker can be selfish and self-centered if a divine connection is not made.

The Divine Connection

A man in one of my seminars sensed the potentially selfish nature of positive self-talk when he raised his hand and challenged, "Lloyd, are you telling me to be conceited?"

"Of course, not," I responded. Conceit means that we define our merits, talents, and attributes by comparing them with those of others. We like ourselves — and believe in ourselves — because we are more attractive, dress better, speak more fluently, perform more consistently, get higher grades, drive a nicer car, or live in a bigger house than our neighbors. Conceited self-talk would have us believe in ourselves only so far as we can surpass other people's achievements, demonstrate greater ability and intelligence, or display bigger and better possessions.

But positive self-talk that leads to and is inspired by a recognition of our self-worth is never self-worship. When we speak positively to ourselves — about ourselves — because we are children of God with inherent worth, our thoughts are never really self-centered. Instead, they demonstrate reverence for the Being who endowed us with that worth. Because our thoughts return to our Father, self-talk that is guided by an awareness of our divine connection is more like a humble prayer for success than a declaration of self-made glory.

No longer is it as challenging to speak positively about ourselves — to ourselves and to others — when we realize that by so doing we demonstrate a love for God. While we may sometimes feel uncomfortable about praising ourselves and believing in our own abilities, if we can think of such positive self-talk as indirectly praising God, giving Him all glory and gratitude, and believing in His stewardship and creations, we begin to make good our divine inheritance of worth.

What Do You Say to You?

Before we can change the tone of our self-talk and transform that self-talk into a more selfless prayer-talk, we must first become *aware* of what kinds of things we are saying to ourselves. Begin by listening to yourself and raising your level of consciousness about your inner monologues. Whether by writing down your inner conversations, saying aloud what you have been thinking, or reminding yourself with a string around your finger or a bean in your shoe, stop and evaluate your thought patterns. Only then can self-talk start to be exchanged for prayer-talk, doubt for hope, and fear for faith.

In *The Feeling Good Handbook,* Dr. David Burns, a psychiatrist at the University of Pennsylvania, outlines ten traps we often fall into while talking to ourselves.

1. All-or-nothing thinking. If a situation isn't perfect, we see it as *total* failure.

2. Over-generalization. We use words like "always" and "never" when we describe ourselves and lose sight of the exceptions.

3. Mental filter. We select one of our weaknesses and concentrate on it, forgetting our more important strengths.

4. Discount the positive. We convince ourselves that our accomplishments are simply a stroke of luck or not really meaningful.

5. Jump to conclusions. We believe things will turn out badly — even when the evidence is neutral.

6. Magnification. We enlarge our problems and shortcomings and minimalize our strengths.

7. Reason emotionally. We interpret our own negative feelings as a sign that we don't deserve happiness.

8. "Should" statements. We motivate ourselves with feelings of obligation and guilt.

9. Label. We fail to deal with specifics and analyze our actions, and as a result, label ourselves inaccurately.

10. Personalize and blame. We accept accountability for situations we actually have no control over.[3]

We all make these kinds of mental mistakes. But when these cognitive traps become habits, we become entrenched in the pits of negative thinking. We find it difficult to lift ourselves out of the mental ruts of self-flagellation — and even self-congratulation. When we rely on the negative motivations of guilt, obligation, bribery, conceit, and fear, our resolution to improve becomes weak and ill-founded. We do things out of a begrudging necessity, which creates short-term resentment and long-term frustration. And if — and when — we no longer feel obligated to improve or are afraid to fail, our motivation to succeed is taken away.

But when we are inspired by a godly perspective on progress, we improve our internal conversation out of a love for God and out of a respect for our internal and eternal worth. As Goethe concluded: "Pleasure is more powerful than the threat of the penalty." An uplifting, God-fearing motivation will always be stronger than the selfish and degrading stimuli of obligation and fear.

Turn to God

During World War II, Captain Eddie Rickenbacker and his seven crewmen were shot down in the middle of the Pacific, with only three small rubber rafts to keep them afloat. Besides being surrounded by sharks, they battled stifling heat — and maddening thirst — during the day, while throughout the night they fought off bitterly cold and uncomfortably wet breezes. Nevertheless, they managed to talk positively to themselves, believing they would somehow survive. Part of their conversation consisted of reading the New Testament together and holding morning and evening prayers.

They were eventually rescued, and Eddie Rickenbacker later said: "I don't wear my religion on my cuff. But it is there, deep. Every night I get down on my knees and thank God for the blessings of the day."[4] Eddie and his crew were able to survive because they looked to God for strength. They filled their minds with positive thoughts and voiced those thoughts to themselves — and to God. They knew that in order to survive, they needed to turn their self-centered and anxious monologues into God-fearing and praising dialogues.

We may not be on a raft in the middle of the Pacific Ocean, but we all do our share of "surviving." We all go through periods when we live from one day to the next, not knowing how we will pay yesterday's bills, meet today's demands, and weather tomorrow's turmoils. When we consider the precariousness of life, the Lord's admonition to the Pharisees comes as comforting counsel: "Men ought always to pray, and not to faint." (Luke 18:1.) In all of His wisdom and foreknowledge, the Lord knew that we would need to do more than just talk to ourselves positively; we would need to "pray always." (Luke 21:36.) We would need to know that Someone would always be listening, that our petitions would always be heard, that we would not just be talking to ourselves, and that we could pray about anything and everything. When we call upon our Heavenly Father, there will not be a busy signal. There is no call-waiting. There is never even a hold button, because He keeps His line open for us, never disconnecting us from His unconditional love and concern.

Tevye talked to himself and to God about everything from his lame horse to his empty pockets to his "lost" daughters. And I believe that God intends for us to do the same. He wants us to intimately involve Him in our lives. No matter how positive our attitude may be, we all need the validation of a listening and loving Ear—always and in "all" ways. Nothing is too small or too great for a sincere prayer directed to a loving Heavenly Father. Positive thinking without reliance on God, without prayer, becomes a selfish attempt to demonstrate our independence. Only when a positive attitude of humble dependence is coupled with faith in God (and voiced in prayer) can real inspiration and empowerment take place.

The Lord teaches in the Sermon on the Mount that our prayers should be heartfelt utterances and not mindless musings: "When ye pray, use not vain repetitions, as the heathen do. . . . Be not ye therefore like unto them: for your Father knoweth what things ye have need of, before ye ask him." (Matthew 6:7–8.) Because the "Father knoweth what things [we] have need of, before [we] ask him," perhaps prayer is more for *us* than for God. We are the ones who benefit most from bending our knees and humbling ourselves in the attitude of prayer. We are the beneficiaries of such spoken (or unspoken) gratitude, desire, repentance, and blessing. Just as positive self-talk helps to align our actions with a better outlook on ourselves and our lives, prayer goes several steps further and gives us a chance to contemplate life from God's divine perspective. As we turn to Him for direction, guidance, and support, we bless our lives with the vision of One who perfectly loves us, knows us, and desires everlasting joy for us.

The Lord's Model for Prayer

Sincere prayer aligns our will with our Father's. Christ's prayer in the Garden of Gethsemane is the perfect example of a completely selfless utterance. Even while taking upon Himself the sins of all mankind and undergoing physical and spiritual pain beyond our comprehension, Christ prayed, "O my Father, if it be possible, let this cup pass from me: nevertheless not as I will, but as thou wilt." (Matthew 26:39.) The Lord's quiet conversation is a hum-

bling demonstration of what it means to really pray. By all
outward appearances, He seemed to be alone, engaging in
a soul-weary monologue. But "for those who have eyes to
see and ears to hear," He was involved in a perfectly selfless
dialogue with God. His "self-talk" was so selfless that He
became one with the Father. "Not as I will, but as thou
wilt" is a perfect demonstration of what it means to take
the "self" out of "self-talk" and to become empowered by
a recognition of divine worth. The contrast between self-
talk and prayer-talk is great indeed:

SELF-TALK	PRAYER-TALK
• I want. I will. • I can. • I need. • I am great. • I am the best.	• Not my will but Thine. • With Thy help, I can. • I desire what is right. • I love Thee and thank Thee for my blessings and success. • I am Thy child, of inherent and infinite worth.

Visualization Becomes Vision

Just as self-talk can be replaced with prayer, the popular
self-improvement practice of visualization evolves into godly
vision when we lose ourselves enough to find ourselves in
the embraces of an all-knowing Father. The theory behind
visualization suggests that we will be successful if we picture
ourselves succeeding. If only we can see ourselves crossing
the finish line, giving a flawless speech, singing a perfectly
pitched song, or responding to stress with control, we will

realize these desired ends. This is what the Music Man (from the Broadway musical) calls "The Think System": if you think you can play a musical instrument, if you can see yourself—and even mentally hear yourself—playing it, you will inevitably play that instrument.

The practice of visualization has much credence. Experimental research and countless personal success stories have proven the theory valid. One of the more famous— and documented—accounts of successful visualization comes from the University of Chicago. Researchers there conducted experiments on three groups of basketball players. The first group practiced no free-throw shots during the month-long experiment. The second group practiced free-throw shots every day. And the third group visualized themselves making free throws every day. When the three groups were tested at the end of the month, the first group showed no improvement. The second group (who had actually practiced) showed a 24-percent improvement. The third group (who had visualized their practice) showed an improvement of 23 percent, only 1 percent less than the second group! In other words, the intense mental practice was nearly as beneficial as the physical workout. (And besides, when you practice in your head, you never miss!)

Positive visualization leads to positive performance. Unfortunately, the reverse is also true: negative visualization undoubtedly leads to negative performance. We see this whenever friends, neighbors, co-workers, or family members call themselves "stupid," "ugly," or "incompetent." And we can discern such negative programming in the subtle turns of their phrases and in the unspoken sentiments of their conversation. A secretary who always complained about her job introduced herself by saying, "I'm *just* a secretary." Because she saw herself as "just" a secretary (and not the intelligent, creative, competent, and contributing person who she was), she was never promoted to another position or seen as more than "just a secretary." A woman in one of my seminars explained this phenomenon well: *"The me I see is the me I'll be."*

We must also realize that others will see us the way we see ourselves. How could we expect it to be otherwise?

When we begin to see ourselves as people who matter (as important parts of the work team, integral members of the family, contributing members of the neighborhood, active participants in church functions, and so on), others will eventually see us that way — and will even help us meet our goals. And then when we come up against certain blind spots along the way, if we believe in something beyond ourselves, if we have vision for our lives, we will be able to move beyond our limitations.

All the while, we must remember that change does not happen overnight. It may be a long, slow process of changing our own as well as others' perceptions of us. It also takes a lot of self-discipline and consistent effort. Positive self-talk and visualization will do no good if we do not prepare, practice, and work — physically, emotionally, mentally, and spiritually. No matter how vividly we envision ourselves playing the piano, if we never sit down and actually put our fingers on the keys, we will never produce beautiful music. The mental and spiritual creation is preliminary to a behavioral and physical creation.

Imagine Walt Disney coming home one day and telling his wife: "Honey, I've got this great idea! I'm going to produce movies and design a wonderful amusement park. And it's all going to center around a mouse named Mickey with a falsetto voice." As far-fetched as such a dream might have sounded to his wife — and to countless others — Walt Disney did what we call dreaming and what he called "imagineering," or creatively engineering and vividly imagining to make seemingly impossible dreams come true.

Several years after Walt Disney died, Disney executives were conducting a tour of Disneyworld when a member of the group bemoaned the fact that Walt never got to see all the spectacular wonders of the amusement park. One of the executives quickly replied: "Oh, but he did. Walt Disney saw all of this in his mind. That's why it's here." And that is how any of us get where we want to be: by visualizing and then acting upon our personal goals, dreams, and visions. As Eleanor Roosevelt put it, "The future belongs to those who believe in their dreams." And as Victor Hugo wrote, "There is nothing like a dream to create the future."

Dreaming and Believing

Believing in a dream — and in God's power to turn dreams into reality — is what Tom Monaghan, the well-known founder of Domino's Pizza, did. Famous for creating a multimillion-dollar pizza enterprise, Monaghan is perhaps less known for his abiding belief in God. Starting out as an orphan at St. Joseph's Home for Boys in Jackson, Michigan, and finally becoming a successful entrepreneur in Ann Arbor, this God-fearing dreamer found strength in the simple but penetrating advice a third grade teacher gave him: "Tom, have faith in God, have faith in yourself — then go do it. *You can be anything you want to be.*" Even though framed photos of him with famous personalities, presidents, politicians, and Pope John Paul II now decorate his walls, the picture most prominently displayed in his office and closest to his heart is of Sister Mary Berarda, the teacher who had faith enough to instill a sense of vision in a young orphan boy. From his inauspicious beginnings, this indomitable dreamer had faith in God and in himself and became "anything [he] want[ed] to be." As a result of his faith, he turned his immature imaginings into fully developed realities.⁵ He started in 1961 with $500 and a dream of delivering pizza in thirty minutes or less. And now his fortune is estimated at $500 million.

Whether we are starting a pizza company, "imagineering" an amusement park, or doing whatever we might need to do to follow our dreams, when our efforts are led by something beyond ourselves, by a compelling vision coupled with good, old-fashioned work, we can reach those once-dreamed-about successes. Isn't it interesting how the harder we work and the more inspiring our dreams become, the "luckier" we get?

Warren Bennis, a respected author and perhaps the country's most renowned leadership consultant, interviewed ninety of the most influential leaders in the country (from both public sector and private corporations). As he looked into their work habits and studied their personal profiles, he expected to find several obvious similarities among them. But he did not. He said of his findings: "The group comprised both left-brain and right-brain thinkers; some who dressed for success and some who didn't; some well-spoken, articulate leaders and some laconic, inarticulate ones; some John Wayne types, and some definitely the opposite. Interestingly, the group included only a few stereotypically charismatic leaders." Then he made the following assertion: "Leaders, then, manage through a *compelling vision* that brings others to a place they have not been before."[6] The one characteristic these leaders had in common was a *compelling vision,* an ability to see beyond the mundane — and beyond themselves.

The Power of Vision

It comes as no surprise then, that one of the most visionary social workers of our time was blind. Famous author and lecturer Helen Keller was blind and deaf from the age of eighteen months. In her later years, when a probing reporter asked her what could be worse than being blind, she responded, "Having eyes to see and no vision."

Civilizations, organizations, families, and individuals depend upon vision, or purposeful imagining and divinely inspired foresight — and have done so since the beginning of time. As soon as we become consumed by the here and now, we lose sight of the vision that will lead us to a more meaningful tomorrow. When we engage only in short-term planning, we never accomplish long-term goals. We never see past the looking-glass that shows us only what we look like, not who we can become.

But what happens to our vision when we enrich it with the empowering awareness that we are children of God?

What happens to our self-perception when, like the prodigal son, we "come to ourselves"? (See Luke 15:11–32.) What dimensions of our character are uncovered when, like Paul, we see with new eyes and our sight is restored? (See Acts 9.) The answers to these questions are a vital part of our living and being, for, as the Proverbs advise, "Where there is no vision, the people perish." (Proverbs 29:18.) How, then, does a recognition of our self-worth transform visualization into godly vision, into purposeful and inspired foresight?

We do all that we can and become all that God would like us to be when we turn to Him for personal vision. When we take time to think about ourselves and our lives from a divine perspective, to discover who we are and why we are here, we catch sight of both the visible — and the invisible, or seemingly impossible — opportunities and responsibilities that are within our stewardship.

Perhaps the most significant difference between visualization and vision comes in the recognition of a God-given purpose — in the uncovering of our larger reasons for being. If we sincerely believe that we are children of God, it follows that He knows us individually, that we have unique identities, and that we each have personalized paths to walk. And when we go through life committed to realizing the measure of our creation, we are better able to develop our inherent talents and to discover our unique attributes. When we not only visualize the success before us but, more important, *envision* the successful life that our Heavenly Father wants for us, we are empowered to step over obstacles and step up to achievements.

This is not to say that life with vision will be easy. Certainly not. Even with inspired foresight, we still come up against challenges and difficulties. But vision will help us see beyond the trials of today and into the hopeful reality of a better day in the future. Vision will help us see the responsible adult in our milk-spilling child, the selfless and loving spouse in the husband or wife who is always late and forgetful, and the more tolerant self in the impatient reflection we may see in the mirror. Vision keeps us moving toward worthy goals even when the pitfalls of life would have us give up and revert to an "easier" way.

As Vance Havner said: "The vision must be followed by the venture. It is not enough to stare up the steps — we must step up the stairs." Visualization would have us imagine and then successfully scale a few of life's carefully selected stairs, while vision allows us to more confidently climb *whatever* steps are before us — even while we catch sight of the eternal staircase, the "big picture," that is before us.

The proverbial story of three bricklayers illustrates the power that comes from seeing more than what is immediately before us. When the first bricklayer was asked what he was doing, he looked up from a pile of bricks, wiped the sweat off his brow, and said, "I am laying bricks." When the second bricklayer was asked what he was doing, he looked up with pride and said, "I am making a strong brick wall." And when the third bricklayer was asked the same question, he resolutely said, "I am building a cathedral."

The first bricklayer did not see beyond his present task. The second visualized a small part of the larger project. But the third *envisioned* the masterwork before him. Because he saw himself as doing something more than just stacking bricks (because he had a vision of the cathedral that would ensue), his efforts had purpose, and he was able to produce greater results. He was not just making a living, he was building a structure that would touch people's lives through the ages.

Imagine the power that would be instilled in our families, companies, and neighborhoods if a compelling and worthy vision directed our lives. When we rear our children with a sense of the higher laws that govern society, they understand that saying no to drugs is saying yes to the thrills of real freedom. When we teach our family that being kind to each other is really an investment in the most lasting sort of friendships, simple courtesies take on more meaning. When we lead our employees to adhere to seemingly inconsequential quality control measures, we produce better products and services (as well as more satisfied customers and more substantial profit sharing). Mundane duties become integral parts of a greater whole. Ultimately, we have more obedient children, more loving families, and more dedicated employees.

Whether we are building a cathedral, a company, a family, or our own self-esteem, when we proceed with vision, our efforts are more closely aligned with our divinely endowed capabilities. We are inspired to reach sometimes even unseen summits of personal growth. When our visualization is enriched with a godly vision, we gradually (and sometimes painfully) scale higher—and steeper—slopes than we previously imagined possible. C. S. Lewis explains such inspired development in terms of a "living house":

Imagine yourself as a living house. God comes in to rebuild that house. At first, perhaps, you can understand what He is doing. He is getting the drains right and stopping the leaks in the roofs, and so on: you knew that those jobs needed doing and so you are not surprised. But presently He starts knocking the house about in a way that hurts abominably and does not seem to make sense. What on earth is He up to? The explanation is that He is building quite a different house from the one you thought of—throwing out a wing here, putting on an extra floor there, running up towers, making courtyards. You thought you were going to be made into a decent little cottage: but He is building a palace.[7]

The Lord never said that in His Father's house are many cottages. Instead He promised His disciples, and each of us, "In my Father's house are many *mansions*"—beautiful, developed, and visionary mansions. (John 14:2; italics added.)

The Light of the World

God sees us as (and shows us how to become) the palatial people who we are and not the pedestrian people we sometimes think ourselves to be, because He is the Light of the World. The Apostle John explained: "God sent not his son into the world to condemn the world; but that the world through him might be saved. . . . And this is the condemnation, *that light is come into the world, and men loved darkness rather than light.*" (John 3:17, 19; italics added.) Men and women may love their own dim-sightedness and fail to find a place in their hearts and minds for the illuminating vision the Light provides.

It is easy to visualize in the dark. We can dream without

distraction: without seeing the obstacles that will cause us to stretch, the rough roads we will have to walk, and the difficult doors we will have to open to enter our mansion. And yet, if we try to reach that palace in the dark, we are sure to trip and fall along the way. But when the Light of the World fills our souls with *vision*, we not only see the mansion prepared for us in all of its intricate detail—a mansion that surpasses our greatest architectural imaginings—but we also walk on a lighted path. (See John 8:12.) When our visualization becomes a divinely inspired vision, we know the Way, the Truth and the Life, and our visionary ventures are channeled by purpose and understanding that is greater than our own. We transcend our personal vision and literally catch sight of the vision that God has for us. God's vision becomes our own.

Visualization that is visionary and self-talk that is prayerful lead to self-improvement that focuses on improvement more than on the self. Christ instructs, "He that findeth his life shall lose it: and he that loseth his life for my sake shall find it." (Matthew 10:39.) When we lose our lives for the Lord's sake, we find the way to real change and lasting improvement. Our selfish success programs become selfless and satisfying services when our God-given worth motivates our efforts, or when we make the divine connection to self-improvement. Whatever self-help practice may invite our attention, whether it be visualization, self-talk, or so many others; when a recognition of our eternal relationship with God illuminates that course of improvement, we will set and achieve goals that are divinely connected to our inherent potential for good.

CHAPTER 7

A DIVINELY INHERITED
PERSONAL MANIFESTO

We are not endeavoring to get ahead of others but only
to surpass ourselves.
                                              —Hugh B. Brown

When I was a child, my father used to chart the growth of
his children on our furnace-room wall. From time to time
he would take us down to the furnace room and mark off
how much we had grown. Especially for the boys, this was
a major event, a ritual remembrance of just how tall (and
thus how "grown up") we were. Sometimes alone with Dad
and sometimes with other family members, we would gather
in the furnace room for the moment of truth.

I remember standing against that wall with all the height
I could muster, straightening my back, lifting my neck, and
even holding my breath until my dad etched a mark in the
wall that corresponded with my "hard-won" height. As soon
as the marking pencil lifted, I would turn around and reflect
on my growth. Sometimes I was elated with the latest de-
marcation; sometimes I was disappointed to see just how
close it was to the last mark; sometimes I wondered if I
would ever be as tall as my older brother and sisters; and

sometimes I was in awe to think I could ever have been so small.

I always talked to my dad about the marks on the wall, and was reassured by his words: "Just a few more years, Lloyd, and you will be up to your full-grown height," he would say. "A couple of years ago you didn't even reach the top of the furnace." "That is the most you have ever grown in one year," he repeatedly assured. I loved this quiet moment of reflection. My father always made me feel tall, even when my growth, compared with that of my siblings, was at times rather minimal. He pointed to the lowest marks on the wall and filled me with encouragement and wonder: "Can you believe you were ever that little? Just think how much more you will grow!" And he was always sure to emphasize the latest — and highest — mark, inspiring me to keep on growing and never to stop stretching. Sometimes he would lift me up and show me how tall I might be "someday."

Eventually, I grew to be as tall as my father. He was as proud as I was of this "accomplishment." He told me that he always knew I would be at least as tall as he was. But he did not need to tell me that. I had felt him believing in my growth from the first times I was measured. He charted my progress not to show me how short — or how tall — I was in a given year but to illustrate how far I had come and how much farther I would be going. The furnace-room wall was not a record of a part of my life; it was a picture of an ever-evolving and increasingly fuller life. Even when the blank portion of the wall was more expansive than the marked portion, its blankness seemed to represent the pos-

sibilities for growth I had yet to discover — possibilities that
my father, from his full-grown height and encompassing
understanding, had always seen fit for me.

Even as an adult, I still go down to that furnace room
occasionally, and though my father is no longer alive, the
principles he taught fall so sweetly upon me as I read the
scribbled markers: "Lloyd at five," "Lloyd at eight," "Lloyd
on his fifteenth birthday." This wall means so much to my
family that even when we recently refinished that portion
of the basement, we could not bring ourselves to paint over
those markings.

The carefully charted wall, in a simple way, has always
served as a lesson in goal-setting for me. It is a picture of
progress, a graphic display of growth. When we set realistic
goals, reflective of this year's marks but still anticipating more
growth, a realization of where we came from and what
heights we can achieve as children of God will round out
our goals with an eternal perspective. (See Romans 8:17.)

A Goal Is Not A Wish

Goal-setting is a necessary part of all self-improvement.
We can best advance from one point in our development
to another when we designate ends, or goals, toward which
our efforts will be directed. A goal is not the same as a
wish. While wishes are hoped for, goals are planned for.
Whether reached in the short term or worked for over a
longer term, goals are an integral part of personal progress,
and help to formulate a personal mission statement or philosophy or creed.

When we set (and write down!) specific goals based on

clearly defined values, we have more control over our lives. We reward ourselves with a sense of direction and a feeling of accomplishment. We fill our lives with the power of purpose. By regularly evaluating our performance, writing down our conclusions, and taking inventory of our goals, short-term commitments turn into lifelong habits. Our goals become magnets that pull us toward the fulfillment of our dreams and align us with the principles that are most dear to us.

While there are probably as many ways to set and achieve goals as there are goals to set, the methods are not as important as the nature of the goals themselves. When we set goals based upon a recognition of our eternal worth, our goals more fully reflect God's goals for us — or our unique potential. The mission statements we write will become personal manifestos, written from the perspective of children of God. Goal-oriented improvement programs will become most effective not just because we have guideposts of improvement but more importantly because those guideposts are in harmony with God's plan for our eternal progress.

How do we decide upon such worthy guideposts? How do we know if our goals are in harmony with such godly purposes as everlasting joy, eternal life, and immortality? How will a recognition of our self-worth help us know what God's goals or desires for us are?

Be Ye Perfect

Just as my father believed I would grow as tall as he was, our Heavenly Father has promised us everything that

He has. And the Lord has pledged, by way of challenge, that we can be even as He is — that we can ultimately become perfect. He did not say, "Be ye therefore okay," "Be ye therefore mediocre," or "Be ye therefore all right." He said, "Be ye therefore *perfect*." (Matthew 5:48; italics added.) Because we can become perfect, "even as [our] Father in heaven is perfect," we most effectively set and reach goals when a recognition of our worth inspires our goal-setting; when, because we realize we have a divine connection to success, we understand how very much God expects from us. We will never achieve perfection in this life, but when we set goals that lead us to strive for perfection, we measure up to the nobility our Father knows we can attain. We take meaningful steps to fulfill the measure of our creation when our goals become God's goals and we become more godlike.

The great Christian writer George MacDonald explains: "Every father is pleased at the baby's first attempt to walk. [And yet], no father would be satisfied with anything less than a firm, free, manly walk in a grown-up son. In the same way, *God is easy to please but hard to satisfy*."[1] While God is *pleased* with every step we take and every inch we grow, He is not *satisfied* with just a single step or with one small inch of development. He still sees the yards of improvement that are ours to achieve — and His to lovingly bequeath. Because He knows we are giants-in-embryo with much growth ahead, He expects us to do all we can with all of the talents and capabilities He has given us.

He knows that growing pains are part of the process and that life sometimes hurts. We all go through painful periods of progress. But how would we know joy if we did not experience pain and sorrow? How would we understand peace if we did not sometimes experience turmoil? We all need to go through certain carefully customized refiner's fires. We all need to have some of our rough edges rounded out. And a recognition of our inherent worth, or, as Norman Vincent Peale calls it, our "untapped, unused potential power," will help us get through those difficult periods. Dr. Peale insightfully observes:

> How . . . do we go about overcoming our obstacles — large or small? First, by realizing who and what you are: the average individual has no idea of the *untapped, unused potential power* within himself.
> Lord Chesterton, an eighteenth century English states-man, said that some people live all their lives and die without ever having their power unleashed. It is a sad fact that all of us are pushed around all our lives by difficulties and obstacles over which we have power — if we will only take and use it. Do you realize who you are? In every one of us, there is a giant; not a pygmy, not a weak little person, but a giant.[2]

When we act on the belief that every time we stretch, the Lord stretches to help us, that every time we fall He can pick us up, we will ultimately become the giants our Father has always seen us as being.

Our Divine Nature

My father's attitude toward the marks on the wall — and toward me — is an instructive example of how our Heavenly Father wants us to set and achieve goals that will lead us to Him — and to become more like Him. Paul taught the Romans that they, and we, are "joint-heirs with Christ," and he informed the Galatians, "Thou art no more a servant, but a son; and if a son, then an heir of God through Christ." (Romans 8:17; Galatians 4:7.) In other words, we have been given a divine inheritance of worth that entitles us to become perfected through Christ, to be joint heirs with Him in the endowment of our Father. The Psalmist explained in the words of the Lord, "I have said, *Ye are gods;* and all of you are children of the most High." (Psalm 82:6; italics added.) Not only can we be the beneficiaries of all the gifts and glories that our Heavenly Father has in store for us, but we can also become like Him because we are literally "children of the most High."

This simple truth that "ye are gods, and all of you are children of the most High" is one of the most empowering understandings of the gospel. Dwight D. Eisenhower affirmed, "I would not lift my little finger to defend the western world against communism if I thought that man were just a machine with no spark of divinity in him."[3] When we change our thought processes and patterns to reflect this truth, our goals will better represent our divine nature. Such a "paradigm-shift," as current usage calls it, changes the way we see ourselves, the nature of our goals, and our methods for achieving those goals. Instead of seeing ourselves as unworthy and even incapable of personal achievement, our shift in thought would have us improve and achieve *because* we have been endowed with the ability to transcend our human tendencies, to realize that our weaknesses are strengths-in-embryo, and that our strengths are developed gifts from God.

Reflection versus Comparison

The important feature in all of this goal-oriented and God-centered improvement is to *reflect* on our progress without *comparing* it to other peoples' successes — and even failures. Reflection is uplifting contemplation, a purposeful and pensive evaluation; while comparison is detrimental judgment, a damaging and misguided perception. Comparison would have us feel "less than" others because our house, our car, our grades, our physical features, and even our bank account are not as good as another's. Or, conversely, comparison would have us feel "greater than" other people if our house, car, grades, and so on are bigger and better than others'. Reflection, however, breeds an attitude of abundance. We glory in others' successes even while we cherish our own (sometimes small and sometimes great) accomplishments. We enjoy the meaningful moments in others' lives and enrich our own special occasions by reflecting on those joyful feelings. Our identity cannot be measured on a comparative scale because it is defined by our *infinite and inherent* worth, a worth that makes any human scale of measurement or comparison seem meaningless.

The furnace-room wall was not an exercise in contrast and comparison. My father made marks on the wall for purposes of reflection — and introspection. It was a place to contemplate my *personal* progress. My marks (or goals) were not based on my siblings' growth patterns but on my own "program" for growth and development.

Just as the furnace-room wall was a reflective rather than a comparative record, the charting of our goals should be

introspective — written to help uncover our divinely endowed abilities. Perhaps that is why journal-writing is so
central to goal-setting. When we write down our goals and
then take personal inventory of our progress, we reflect on
our efforts and have a chance to evaluate ourselves — against
ourselves and by ourselves. We compare our improvement
with our own development, and our achievements become
inspired by a recognition of our potential and our worthiness
to achieve.

This is not to say that learning about the accomplishments of others is not beneficial — and even essential. Some
of my favorite books are biographies and autobiographies.
I love to read about peoples' lives, to glory in their successes
and learn from their mistakes. I am encouraged and
strengthened by the stories of such great people as David
O. McKay, Spencer W. Kimball, Mother Teresa, Winston
Churchill, C. S. Lewis, and Helen Keller. I *reflect* on their
accomplishments and am inspired by their greatness. My
spirits are lifted for days after reading their accounts. I try
not to compare my own life with theirs, but I do enhance
my living with the story of their lives.

Perhaps the most beneficial reflection in which we can
engage is reflecting on the life of Christ. Is there any more
inspiring way to work improvement into our lives than by
filling our minds and hearts with the story of the Master
Improver, the Means for improvement? Certainly such enabling reflection comes nowhere near the pitfalls of comparison.

Divine Discontent versus Devil's Dissonance

Elder Neal A. Maxwell succinctly explains the difference between Godly reflection and damaging comparison: "We can distinguish more clearly between divine discontent and the devil's dissonance, between dissatisfaction with self and disdain for self. We need the first and must shun the second, remembering that when conscience calls to us from the next ridge, it is not solely to scold but also to beckon."[4]

Reflection is analogous to what Elder Maxwell calls "divine discontent," or an impetus to improve that is based on our feelings of worth as children of God. Comparison is more like the "devil's dissonance," or a dissatisfaction with self that arises from feelings of inadequacy and even unworthiness. "Devil's dissonance" would have us respond to the Lord's invitation to "be . . . perfect" with feelings of inferiority and thoughts of doubt. We might be discouraged by such an invitation because we feel undeserving of the Lord's blessings — and even of His atoning sacrifice. But when our conscience calls for improvement *because* we know we can do and be better, because we know our Heavenly Father expects more from us and will bless us to achieve it, this "divine discontent" leads us to set goals that reflect our self-worth.

A Personal Manifesto

This kind of reflection inspires us to define our lives' purposes, to look to God and change our thinking to match His reasons for our being.

Just as any successful organization prepares a corporate mission statement that reveals a company's values (what is most important to the company, its reason for being, and its sense of direction), we would all benefit from designing a personal manifesto — a written declaration of our values, motives, and goals.

Xerox Corporation has an informal mission statement: "Quality means providing our external and internal customers with innovative products and services that fully satisfy their requirements. Quality improvement is the job of every Xerox employee." For Xerox, quality products and services are the object of their greatest estimation.

Bonneville International Corporation similarly promises "to provide personal growth opportunities for employees, to enhance the effectiveness, power, influence, and value of properties, and to exert positive leadership in the broadcast industry." In a sentence, the company's values and vision are presented.

Wendy's restaurants have a clearly developed sense of who they are and what they are about. The mission statement displayed on the wall of each Wendy's restaurant includes these words: " . . . to serve the freshest quality products as quickly and efficiently as possible. Quality is our recipe." From Xerox to Bonneville to Wendy's, corporations of all sizes and interests declare their procedures and purposes in concise and meaningful mission statements. They present their goals publicly; by so doing, they hope to better align their decisions with their values. The result is a more unified corporation moving in a clearly defined direction.

Just as a well-defined mission statement can give a company a sense of direction and purpose, a "personal manifesto," a concise statement of our value-oriented goals, can guide our decisions and clarify our intentions. A manifesto is not a description (or a rundown of height, weight, and hair color); neither is it just one goal ("I want to be president of my company"). Instead, a personal manifesto defines us in the way the Constitution defines the United States: it reveals what is of ultimate significance in our lives. It represents our vision of the future, translates that vision into a direction, and states what we are committed to do in order to realize that vision.

In writing a personal manifesto, we clarify the purpose of our life and identify our unique essence. An example of a personal manifesto might include something as simple as this: "I will be honest, loyal, and sensitive to my family and friends; I will bring quality to the tasks I perform." Or this: "My mission is to love God, myself, and others. I will seek to learn from past experiences and grow by taking prudent risks and taking responsibility for my life. I will invest in myself and in others by placing value in people and relationships, not in things and programs." Whatever form a personal manifesto might take, it need not be written in permanent ink, as it will probably change several times in a lifetime. A changing personal manifesto documents growth and is a healthy demonstration of the evolution of our character. Writing several drafts and sharing them with trusted friends will provide added insights and extra motivation.

Abraham Lincoln wrote the following creed:

> I believe in God, the Almighty Ruler of nations, our

great and good merciful Maker, our Father in Heaven, who notes the fall of a sparrow and numbers the hairs on our heads. I recognize the sublime truth announced in the Holy Scriptures and proved by all history that those nations are blessed whose God is the Lord. I believe that the will of God prevails. Without him, all human reliance is vain. With that assistance I cannot fall. I have a solemn vow registered in heaven to finish the work I am in, in full view of my responsibility to God, with malice toward none; with charity for all; with firmness in the right, as God gives me to see the right.

Mahatma Gandhi penned this powerful resolution:

Let . . . our first act every morning be to make the following resolve for the day:
I shall not fear anyone on earth.
I shall fear only God.
I shall not bear ill toward anyone.
I shall not submit to injustice from anyone.
I shall conquer untruth by truth.
And in resisting untruth I shall put up with all suffering.

The most meaningful way to formulate such a manifesto is to write it on the basis of our God-given worth. The very act of writing goals that reflect our self-worth forces a succinct expression of our deepest beliefs, heartfelt aspirations, and worthy goals. A personal manifesto should be:

1. Comprehensive: Does it include *all* of your roles — father, mother, son, daughter, neighbor, supervisor, and so on — and all of your interests?

2. Practical: Can it really be lived by?

3. Inspiring: Will it require stretching? Does it make the divine connection?

Such a manifesto will be a great source of wisdom, power, and guidance.

The Family Manifesto

Just as corporations and individuals can benefit from documenting their mission, families can also derive strength from a clear presentation of their purpose. Whether representing a single-parent, widowed, or traditional household, a family manifesto that is prominently displayed on a wall or concisely written in a family scrapbook or journal reaffirms to family members their collective purpose and confirmed goals. (And visitors who happen upon such a statement reinforce the family's vision for itself with sincere questions and exterior support.) Family members can derive strength and solidarity from a manifesto like this one: "We are committed to the development, growth, and happiness of each family member, helping them discover their worth and fulfill their potential. Our family will reinforce each others' independent abilities, teach each member of his or her interdependent responsibilities, and give them freedom and encouragement to develop their unique, individual talents." Who could help but take pride in the direction and bask in the security of such a statement? And perhaps most important, who could help but feel the unity such a declaration might bring?

Such a manifesto is made stronger when each member of the family develops his or her personal manifesto. Each individual manifesto feeds into and complements the family manifesto. An organization is only as strong as its individual members. And the personal manifesto becomes the source of strength and vision that it should be when written with an awareness of our self-worth — when written from the perspective of a child of God.

Self-improvement ideologies have suggested the writing of a goal sheet or something like a mission statement for years. Certainly, this is not an innovative practice. But when mission statements are written with the understanding that we have already been given a divine manifesto, when mission statements are divine-centered and worth-inspired personal manifestos, this time-honored practice takes on much more meaning.

An Eternal Birthright

How might our vision for ourselves change when we define our goals around the knowledge of an eternal birthright? How might our goals better reflect our potential when we recognize our capabilities as God's offspring? *How might the rest of our manifesto read if the first, unalterable line stated, "I am a child of God, and because of that abiding truth . . . "?*

Paul suggested the power of such an awareness when he preached to the Athenians about the "unknown God": "In him we live, and move, and have our being; as certain also of your own poets have said, *For we are also his offspring.*" (Acts 17:28; italics added.) When we understand that because we are God's children "we live and move," our lives become more than just an existence. When we realize that our divine parentage has given us our "being," we truly can be all we were meant to become. When we set goals that are founded on correct principles, we adhere to values that will show us the way, shower us with more truth and light, and give meaning to our lives. When a personal manifesto is written as a declaration of our self-worth, we inscribe a godly vision for our lives. Beyond the marks on the furnace-room walls of our own dream houses, our goals become markings on the walls of the mansions that God has prepared for us. And this greater understanding, while giving us more of an eternal vision and uncovering more of our infinite opportunities, also inspires a deeper sense of responsibility about our actions, thoughts, and lives.

. . . .

CHAPTER 8

NO MORE EXCUSES

The acceptance of total responsibility for our lives is the chief hallmark of mature human beings. The acceptance of responsibility means that from then on in life, we have no more excuses.

—Brian Tracy

Agency, or the right we have as human beings to choose, is perhaps the most fundamental principle upon which self-improvement depends. Because we are not totally determined by our genes, our environment, our childhood, our aptitudes, or even by our mistakes, we have the ability to mold ourselves and our lives according to our own choices. We have the ability to improve and develop because we have the ability to choose: to decide whether we will exercise or not, whether we will read or not, whether we will listen or not, whether we will relax or not. And this recognition of our agency is one of the greatest facilitators for change. When we really come to know that because we are children of a loving God we can *choose* to change, we *will* more readily change—and become like Him.

Agency and Self-Worth

God, in His infinite wisdom and foreknowledge, did not send us to earth as clones, programmed for perfection — or for damnation — with fixed fates and determined destinies. Instead, He sent us as agents unto ourselves, fully equipped to work out our own salvation through the redeeming sacrifice of His Son. While He did not make the choices for us, He endowed us with all that we would need to make good choices: a perfect Model, a personal Savior, a keen conscience (to sense the disparity between right and wrong), self-awareness (the ability to evaluate our own thoughts, feelings, and actions), and an unchanging and infinite worth. All of these components for the effective use of our agency may sound familiar, except perhaps the inclusion of self-worth. Why would a recognition of our self-worth be fundamental to making good choices? How does self-worth influence the way we make decisions?

The more we become aware of our divinely endowed worth, the better we can accept responsibility for our choices — and the more responsible our choices will be. Self-worth serves as an equalizer for both the good and the bad choices we make: while a bad choice may (at least partially) damage our self-esteem and a good choice fortify it, neither a bad nor a good choice can affect our self-worth. This inherent, unchanging worth withstands all the buffetings of our agency and can help us to achieve more of an equilibrium with regard to our self-esteem. As a result, we can more fully accept responsibility for our lives because we know that despite the bad — and even outside of the good —

decisions that we make (or have made), our self-worth remains constant.

The Power to Choose

One effect of realizing this steady force inside of us is that we need not put ourselves at the mercy of outside and negative influences. We need not be chameleons who take upon ourselves the moods and natures of the people around us and the situations in which we find ourselves. Because we have personal claim to an infinite and unchangeable worth, we are our own best agents for everything from moods to attitudes to actions. Ultimately, we are the ones who have to decide how we feel, what we think, and what we do.

Many years ago I gained an insight into this empowering principle of agency while working for a man I will call Bill. Bill was a business executive who had successfully risen to a place of financial security and prominent social status. Bill was a leader in the office, in the company, and in the community, and I was his "right-hand man."

I usually got to work before Bill, and I would be at my desk writing, typing, or phoning when he walked in. "Hello, Bill. It's nice to see you. Good morning," was my usual greeting. Often he would grumble: "Good morning? What's good about it?" Then he would storm into his office and slam the door, and I would slouch in my chair and say to myself: "Bill is in a bad mood. Okay then, I am in a bad mood. It is going to be a bad day." And it was a bad day. Other times Bill was cheerful: "Lloyd, hello. How are you? It sure is nice to see you today." On these occasions, I would straighten my back, look out the window with a smile, and think: "Bill is in a good mood. Great! I am in a good mood. It is going to be a good day." And it was a good day. If Bill was in a good mood, somehow I was in a good mood. But if Bill was upset and grumpy, somehow I began to feel upset and grumpy.

In effect, I was allowing Bill to determine what kind of day I would have. My boss who controlled my work assignments was also controlling my thoughts, my actions, my feelings — my day. I soon learned that a life based on the weaknesses — or even on the strengths — of others is a roller-coaster ride in "non-response-ability." One day I would be feeling up because my boss was up, and the next day I would be feeling down because he was down. I was not taking responsibility for my own emotions and attitudes. I was not controlling my own thoughts and responses, following my own course of action and accounting for the choices I made. I was not using my safety belt of worth to stabilize my life and keep myself from being affected by the jolts and jarrings of my boss's behavior. Instead, I was being driven from the hill of Bill's positive response to the valley of his negative reaction — without doing enough of my own steering along the way. I let Bill put his hands on the steering wheel of my life and his foot on the gas pedal of my progress.

Fortunately, life is a process of change, growth, and maturity. And I made a few attitudinal changes that brought a greater sense of control to my work and more fulfillment to my life. I realized that I (and every other human being) was *worthy* of better treatment and could respond with more mature and responsible behavior. While I could not change his feelings or his behavior, I could change *my* reaction to it. While facing the fact that Bill was a negative influence in my life, I *chose* to respond to Bill more positively. I wanted to choose for myself what kind of day I would have. And this experience (at least in part) taught me that the ability to choose is what positive and responsible thinking and behaving depend upon — and what Christianity teaches.

Our Own Barometer of Behavior

While popular self-improvement literature might call such behavior "proactivity," Paul and the disciples of Christ would call it "walk[ing] by faith," or making decisions, as Paul continued, "not by sight." (2 Corinthians 5:7.) We make choices every time we wake up, open the blinds, or pull the drapes. If the sun is shining or if a haze is settling or if the rain is pouring or if the snow is falling, we have the power to choose what kind of day we will have — no matter what the weather may be like. We can walk as if the sun were on our shoulders even when the sky is overcast. We become our own personal forecasters and can determine our own "emotional, attitudinal, and spiritual weather." With a warm heart and a calm disposition, we can remain unaffected by the cold and stormy weather outside. But all too often our mood is a function of the climate or of the social environment (or, for me, of my boss's mood). Just because it is bleak outside or gloomy in the office or stressful at home does not mean we need to be bleak, gloomy, and stressed inside.

We have the power to see "not by sight" but with Godly vision, to walk by faith because we are the beneficiaries of

Christ's guiding light. As children of God, we are endowed with a conscience that highlights the distinction between right and wrong. Because God gave His Son as the Light of the World, and because we are all blessed with the ability to choose between dark and light, wrong and right, we too can be lights in the world. (John 8:12.) No matter what religion we may be, we are all born with the light of Christ, or a conscience. While sin may dim that light, somewhere deep inside, it is still shining. And the more we align our lives with Christ-like ideals, the more the Light of the World will grow and shine in us, and the more we can choose to radiate a happy countenance and a cheerful disposition.

One of the greatest blessings of Christ's perfect and unwavering light is that it maintains our agency and empowers us with responsibility: the light of Christ allows us to make choices even on a darkened day. Just as a beacon of light cuts through the dark of night, the light of Christ allows us to see even through the fog of human fallibility. The Lord Himself explained: "A city that is set on a hill cannot be hid. Neither do men light a candle, and put it under a bushel, but on a candlestick; and it giveth light unto all that are in the house. *Let your light so shine before men, that they may . . . glorify your Father which is in heaven.*" (Matthew 5:14–16; italics added.)

Whenever we choose to act according to our conscience, and to let our "light so shine," we glorify our Father in Heaven and light the eternal flame of worth that He gave us — and that may be lying dormant within us. We make claim to the universal birthright of worth that facilitates all decision-making. Our self-worth is the candlestick upon which the candle of our agency rests, and we are the responsible illuminators. Will we draw upon the light of Christ and become empowered by our worth, or will we stay in the self-evading dark? Will we let our light shine, or will we be consumed by the darkness around us?

Never Be SNIOP

A middle-aged woman I met at a seminar in Richard's Bay, South Africa, taught me a great lesson. She came to talk to me during a break between sessions, and with tears in her eyes she showed me a piece of paper on which someone had written "Never be SNIOP." A friend had given her the piece of paper when the woman was in the hospital, lying flat on her back, and believing — as the doctors had prognosticated — that she would never walk again. Her friend had explained the meaning of the cryptic message: "Never be Subject to the Negative Influence of Other People." The message made a real impact on her life.

She began to believe this faith-promoting thought and feel the power that came from carrying her own "weather" around with her. She was not going to let the "experts" rain on her life; she was not going to let her associates fog up the windows of her career. She recalled with great resolve: "If I had listened to the doctors, I would never have walked again. If I had listened to some of my 'friends' and co-workers, I would never have been where I am. I would have given up a long time ago."

Now she is a happy, healthy, and productive office manager because she knows that taking responsibility for her life is prerequisite to really living. She refused to let the attitudinal and emotional climate in the hospital, in the office, and even in her home, control her. Instead, she created her own atmosphere of positive influence.

At another seminar in another part of the world, a group of seminar participants responded to this idea of "climate control" in a completely different way. As is often the case in a hotel conference room, the temperature was too cool. I usually have difficulty determining whether or not the temperature is comfortable for the participants, because while I am up and moving around, they are sitting still and are not as affected by their own body heat. So on this occasion, when we took a break and mingled in the hallway, I heard several people complaining about the frigid temperature — and my insensitivity to it. They could not see me around the corner, and they conversed loudly, without knowing that I could hear their complaints. With sweat trickling down my own face, I was rather surprised at their remarks:

"It is so cold in there. We should do something; we should tell Lloyd."

"I don't know. I just know I am freezing!"

"Look, feel my hands — they're frozen."

"My feet are numb."

"Any minute we'll be able to see our breath."

"What do you think we should do?"

Finally, one woman summarized their discussion with this ironic remark: "Well, *he should just know* that it is cold!"

In a seminar on proactivity and personal responsibility, this woman had responded with a typically reactive statement. Instead of approaching me and asking if there was anything that could be done to change the temperature in the room, this woman sat back and decided to further impede her learning by just "deciding to freeze." She was not taking personal responsibility for her comfort; she was expecting me to be her personal mind (and body) reader. I would have been more than glad to have the hotel staff adjust the temperature, but I first had to know that it needed to be altered.

Actors, Not Reactors

While the woman in the seminar in Richard's Bay refused to let conditions and conditioning control her life, these people—in a minor way—were letting the climate impede their opportunities for learning. They were being reactors instead of actors, passive onlookers instead of active participants. Taking responsibility for our lives is a vital element in developing our self-esteem and an empowering benefit of realizing our self-worth.

When we are secure enough in our relationship with God that we believe in our inherent worth, we will feel more secure about taking action and more confident in making decisions. Our approach to problem-solving and conflict-management will be more assertive and proactive. We will not worry so much about what our associates may say and what the doctor might do—and even what Lloyd might think about adjusting the room temperature. Instead, we can fashion our day and our life according to the controls of our inner self—a self that is defined by our God-given worth. We will not aggressively take charge and offend other people but will assertively take responsibility for our lives and our circumstances.

The key to being responsible for our own lives is in making decisions from the inside out. When we look deep inside ourselves for direction, we will be led by the light of Christ and more attuned to the whisperings of our conscience. We will become more aware of our self-worth and, as a result, make decisions that build our self-esteem.

At times we are tempted to disobey our inner promptings, to submit to selfishness and pride. But if we disobey, we deny our deepest natures as children of God, and we lose the self-respect that comes from self-mastery.

Living from the inside out brings a constancy into our lives, no matter what our circumstances. It enables us to realize that, as God's children, we have a stewardship over our lives—over our bodies, our time, our talents, our possessions, and our relationships with others and with ourselves.

Inside-out living teaches us humility as we learn to depend on the Lord. And it teaches us gratitude for His constant care and support, and for His own example of inside-out living.

Choices and Consequences

In the New Testament story of Mary and Martha, Mary chose to live from the inside-out. She made her own decision about how she would spend her day. Luke records that when the Savior "entered into a certain village, . . . a certain woman named Martha received him into her house. . . . But Martha was cumbered about much serving, and came to him, and said, Lord, dost thou not care that my sister hath left me to serve alone? bid her therefore that she help me." (Luke 10:38,40.) Martha seemed irritated that her sister Mary "sat at Jesus' feet, and heard his word" (v. 39) while she was busy preparing the repast.

The Savior's answer to Martha's task-oriented inquiry is a lesson in choice and accountability. He simply replied, "One thing is needful: and Mary hath *chosen* that good part, which shall not be taken away from her." (V. 42; italics added.) Mary's choice to learn more about the gospel of Christ was "that good part which shall not be taken away from her." Martha's choice was to be "careful and troubled about many things" rather than to learn at the Lord's feet.

It seems that the Lord was not just teaching Martha about the eternal nature of the gospel, "that good part which shall not be taken away," but was perhaps just as significantly instructing her on the eternal principle of agency: we cannot choose without simultaneously choosing consequences. For example, we can choose whether or not we will jump from an airplane, but we cannot choose what will happen to us once we jump. Consequences are based on natural laws that cannot be defied. We may not recognize certain consequences as the flip-side of our choice; consequences may be clothed in some other raiment than what we expected them to wear. But they are nevertheless there and are always a function of our decisions.

We Are Responsible

Just as Mary and Martha made different choices with different consequences, we are constantly making choices for which we must accept the consequences. Responsible people who are interested in meaningful self-improvement will not blame others for the consequences of their choices. They will realize that they are their own stewards who ultimately must answer to God for that stewardship. Reactive statements like "My boss didn't like me so I didn't get the promotion," "My kids are making me miserable," "I can't help it," "The devil made me do it," and "I've never been any good at math since I had that terrible algebra teacher in high school" will be replaced by more proactive and positive pronouncements. The language of the reactive loser has no place in the responsible, proactive winner's vocabulary because he or she believes in a God-given birthright — an inheritance of worth that demands accountability.

A graphic illustration of the difference in language between those who really understand their self-worth and those who do not is instructive:

WITHOUT SELF-WORTH	WITH SELF-WORTH
• I will not and cannot change. • I am unforgivable. • I am unworthy. • I am my mistakes. • It is not my fault.	• I am a changing person. • I can be forgiven. • I am worthy of God's blessings. • I learn and grow from my mistakes. • I am responsible.

For the Christian, it is not enough to explain away faults or minimize negative tendencies with statements like "That's just the way I am," "I'm not a morning person," or "That's what always happens to me," because anyone who believes in Christ must ultimately believe in his or her worth — and subsequent potential — as a beneficiary of the atonement. Those who defer responsibility are not only offending their own value, but, more important, they are offending Him who created them, Him who endowed them with that worth, Him who blessed them with the means to repent and to return to Him. When we think and act in such a way that denies our self-worth, when we believe we are not "response-able," we insult God with underestimations of His creations and of His plan for our salvation.

As the popular saying goes, "God didn't make no junk." So if for no other reason, taking responsibility and avoiding personal scapegoats is the correct and worthy thing to do because it gives deference to our Creator. It reveals our belief that God really did not make any junk. And while dysfunctions, disabilities, and disadvantages continue to complicate these issues of blame and accountability, if we will remember that God has different levels of expectations for each of us and that we all answer to varying degrees of responsibility, we will better understand the importance of doing all that we can with what we *do* have. C. S. Lewis explained it this way:

> To judge the management of a factory, you must consider not only the output but the plant. Considering the plant at Factory A it may be a wonder that it turns out anything at all; considering the first-class outfit at Factory B, its output, though high, may be a great deal lower than it ought to be. No doubt the good manager at Factory A is going to put in new machinery as soon as he can, but that takes time. In the meantime low output does not prove that he is a failure.[1]

Where much is given, much is expected; what is put

into a factory in large measure determines what is expected to come from that factory. Where misfortune and malady mark our path, our Heavenly Father's expectations (and our own accountability) are adjusted accordingly.

Acknowledge God in All Things

Giving credit where credit *is* due is important in developing responsible attitudes and taking charge of our lives. Frequently, when our lives take a turn for the better and we are filled with newfound hope and blessings, we ascribe our successes to hard work or happenstance and thank the stars that "lady luck" found her way to our doorstep. But this sort of deferment is just as void of God-fearing responsibility.

When we are blessed with bounty and success, if we fail to acknowledge God as the giver of all that is good, we demonstrate false security and look to inferior sources of strength. One of the greatest manifestations of responsibility is gratitude — to God and others for the good things of life. Ironically, we seem to more readily turn to God when bad things happen, and we frequently forget Him while we enjoy the very blessings that He has sent our way. When we recognize the good things of life as blessings from God, we become responsible stewards and godly caretakers. We take better care of ourselves and our lives when we realize that our lives are not just our own — when we believe that we are on God's errands, we are His instruments, and our successes are His glories.

This principle is explained in a humorous and heartwarming way in the classic film *Shenandoah* when Jimmy

Stewart, a widowed Virginian farmer, gathers his family to say grace on the food. Feeling a bit uncomfortable about even offering a prayer, the farmer honors his deceased wife by carrying on the Christian tradition: "Lord, we cleared this land. We plowed it, sowed it, and harvested. We cooked the harvest. It wouldn't be here, we wouldn't be eating it, if we hadn't done it all ourselves. We worked dogbone hard for every crumb and morsel, but we thank you just the same anyway, Lord, for this food we are about to eat. Amen." Even though the farmer's gratitude seems a bit half-hearted, in his own way he gives credit where it is due. If with nothing else than the actual gesture of bowing his head and leading his family in an all too dutiful prayer, he makes an effort to thank the Lord for the bounties they enjoy. And he demonstrates a certain amount of responsibility and humility (minimal though it may be) by even saying a prayer, or by attempting to give credit where — at least his deceased wife would say — it is supposed to be due.

Even though the Shenandoah farmer and many of us might struggle to understand how works without faith can be dead, if we start by doing no more than just going through the motions of prayer, we will see how our lives take on deeper meaning as we begin to recognize the Lord's hand in all that we do. Taking action and being responsible are by-products of agency, and agency — like worth — is a gift from God, an integral component of the decision-making process that leads to self-improvement. When we realize that we have inherent worth as children of God, we make better use of the agency He has blessed us with: we begin acting instead of reacting, we begin to walk by faith and "not by sight." We, like the apostles of Christ who minister in His name, must look to God in order to fully take charge of our lives and to take responsibility for our choices. The book of Acts repeatedly reminds us that only when Peter and the other disciples wholeheartedly accepted the "consequences" of their choice to follow Christ did they stop denying Him and really start acting in His name: healing the sick, preaching to the poor in spirit, and spreading the good news of the gospel. In the same way, when we wholeheartedly accept the responsibility that our God-given worth gives us and that our dependence on Deity prescribes for us, we will uncover the opportunities for development that are uniquely ours. Only then will we realize our personal best.

. . . .

CHAPTER 9

OUR PERSONAL BEST

I do the very best I know how — the very best I can; and
I mean to keep doing so until the end.
— Abraham Lincoln

This section on *intra*personal development has discussed
"becoming all that we are meant to become," "discovering
our inherent and infinite capabilities," not comparing our
progress with others, or, quite simply, *doing our personal
best*. As the many examples, scriptures, and success stories
have demonstrated, these are not empty words. Each of us
really can improve and, ultimately, realize our God-given
potential. The process of growth is usually long and sometimes challenging, but we all have a divine endowment of
agency, the ability to make choices and to work meaningful
change in ourselves and in our lives.

Before we proceed with a discussion of *inter*personal
success, we need to remind ourselves of the principles that
make all of this personal progress possible. We need to briefly
review and more closely examine how a recognition of our
self-worth is the operative precept upon which lasting improvement depends. As we define what it means to do our
personal best, put this book to the test and begin to witness

for yourself how a deeply internalized self-worth kindles a quiet explosion of personal power.

The Parable of the Talents

One of the Savior's explanations of doing our personal best comes to us in the parable of the talents. In the twenty-fifth chapter of Matthew, the Lord likens the kingdom of heaven to a "man travelling into a far country, who called his own servants, and delivered unto them his goods." (V. 14.) He had three servants among whom he divided his inheritance. To the first he gave five talents; to the second he gave two talents; and to the last he gave a single talent.

When the master returned from his travels, the servant who had received five talents "came and brought other five talents, saying, Lord, thou deliveredst unto me five talents: behold, I have gained beside them five talents more." (V. 20.) And the master responded: "Well done, thou good and faithful servant: thou hast been faithful over a few things, I will make thee ruler over many things: enter thou into the joy of thy lord." (V. 21.) So the servant with five talents doubled his stewardship, and the lord rewarded him by making him "ruler over many things."

The same sort of recompense took place between the second servant and the lord. This servant reported to his returned master: "Lord, thou deliveredst unto me two talents: behold, I have gained two other talents beside them." (V. 22.) And the master replied in kind: "Well done, good and faithful servant: thou has been faithful over a few things, I will make thee ruler over many things: enter thou into the joy of thy lord." (V. 23.) The second servant received the same reward as the first servant, even though the first servant made a return of five talents and the second servant increased the lord's holdings by two talents. Both servants doubled their allotment of talents, and because of their faithful and responsible stewardship, the lord made them rulers over many things.

Despite the fact that they started out with a different number of talents, they each received the same reward because they had done their *personal* best with these holdings. What they *did* with the money their master gave them was more important than the actual amount of money by which they increased his holdings.

The same principle applies to the development of our talents, or to the stewardship God has given us over our individual abilities. Whether we were given five talents or twenty, one talent or ten (monetary or otherwise) is not as important as what we do with those talents. As Peter said, "God is no respecter of persons," and because we are of equal and unchanging worth to our Father, He will reward us commensurate with our efforts, on a customized — and even personalized — scale of improvement and not in accordance with any overt measurement of success. (See Acts 10:34.) Whether we were born in a ghetto or near a country club, on the streets or in a loving home, in disease and poverty or in health and wealth, because we all have the same worth, we can all earn the same heavenly reward. God is interested in our individual performance on our own stage of ability and experience, and whether our acts have been in our own backyard or the object of public applause, we will be accountable only for those talents, privileges, and opportunities that *have* been given to us.

Because an equal endowment of worth has been given to all of God's children, we are all expected to do the most with what we have — in the best way we can. Our personal bests will all be different, but they will universally reflect our unchanging and infinite worth.

When Jesse Jackson was running for president in 1984, I was assigned to cover one of his political rallies for the local TV station. The audience was mesmerized by the inspiring message of his speech. Jesse Jackson repeatedly said, "You may have been born in the ghetto, but the ghetto does not have to be born in you." And he had his audience chant, "I am somebody!" No matter where we come from or what mistakes we have made or what limitations we may endure, "I am somebody" is the electrifying chant of his rallies and the unspoken message of this timeless parable.

You may have heard the same idea in these terms: No *body* is a *nobody*. We are all somebody to the Lord. The talents we may or may not have do not make us worthy or unworthy of the Lord's blessings. Righteous individual stewardship and personal development of those talents with which we are blessed will allow us to enter into the joy of our Lord.

The parable goes on to explain that the one thing that keeps us from having our talents added upon is the failure to develop our God-given abilities — no matter how apparently weak or strong they may be. The third servant with one talent had just as good a chance as the other servants at being made a "ruler over many things," but fear dictated his stewardship. He explained to the lord: "I was afraid, and went and hid thy talent in the earth." (Matthew 25:25.) Faith in himself and in his lord was replaced by the fear of losing what little he had. As a result, the master called him an unprofitable servant, a "wicked and slothful servant" (v. 26), and gave his one talent to the servant with ten, the servant who had already proven his stewardship.

Fear and Faith

The last servant did not achieve his personal best because fear instead of faith motivated his improvement. He was afraid to lose what he had because he did not recognize what he had already been given: a divinely endowed worth that was full of potential and characterized by possibilites. Elder Marvin J. Ashton explained that this sort of self-defeat is the most disappointing — for ourselves and for others: "How sad, how long the day when we become low on ourselves. The worst form of defeat is to be conquered by self. Defeat is not pleasant, but nothing is so painful and devastating as self-defeat. A person is poor when he places despair over hope."[1]

Just a few steps removed from despair is fear, the fear of failure — and sometimes even the fear of success. Such self-doubt or fear was the cause of the third servant's failure and remains at the root of most of our disappointments, both large and small.

The implications of this parable are far-reaching. If we look to self-help books and other self-improvement sources because we are *afraid* of losing our job, afraid of losing our spouse, afraid of failing as a parent, afraid of not realizing our own hopes and dreams, afraid of who we really are, then our efforts to improve will be swallowed by fear and buried in self-doubt. Any advancement that takes place will only be a cosmetic improvement that attempts to hide uncertainty; it will not be an "inside-out" remedy that brings our divine worth to the surface. Heavenly Father will not make us a ruler over more things if we rule ourselves and our lives on the basis of fear. When a faith in God—and a belief in our God-given worth—motivates our improvement, we will reap the rewards of a responsible stewardship.

All too often we proceed upon the basis of past mistakes, yesterday's failures, and unfulfilled desires. We carry emotional and psychological baggage that weighs us down and prevents us from exploring and developing the unique abilities that God has given us. Psychologists call such living "gunny sacking," or carrying around negative mental sacks that are full of disappointments, marked by failures, and colored with fears. But when we believe in God enough to believe that we are His children—endowed with inherent worth—we can begin to let go of this baggage and feel the lightness of His love. We will look at talents as blessings, as opportunities for personal development, and not as dreadful responsibilities that (like the third servant) we would rather hide in the earth.

What's Right with You?

This kind of mindset has become glaringly apparent to me as I have conducted a certain "strengths-and-weaknesses" exercise in hundreds of seminars with thousands of different people all around the world. At a certain point in my presentation, I will stop and ask the participants to take two minutes to write down ten of their strengths. "What's right with you? What do you like about you?" I ask. Without fail, whenever I make this request, the men and women squirm in their chairs and rack their brains in order to make a list of ten good things about themselves. They struggle and strain and usually cannot come up with more than a few strong points. Immediately thereafter, I ask them to write down ten of their weaknesses, things they would like to change about themselves. Almost reflexively they can make their list of ten (and sometimes even a few extra) weaknesses in just a moment. With time to spare, they often turn to their neighbors and compare their lists of weaknesses, complaining about their inadequacies and wishing they could be like someone else.

A verbal rendition of this exercise elicits the same response. In smaller groups where there is more familiarity between participants, I ask the men and women to turn to their neighbors for sixty seconds and verbally share their strengths with this assigned listener. Often the exercise begins with extended silence; then that silence turns into giggles and sighs and expressions of "I don't know. I just can't think of anything." But during the next sixty seconds when I ask them to share some of their weaknesses with their neighbors, the room fills with chatter, and an immediate sort of bonding seems to take place between speaker and listener. They have so much more to talk about.

The Divine Connection

Something as simple as how we present ourselves to other people or how we accept a compliment also reveals the degree to which a divine connection to our self-perception has been made. If someone tells us that we look nice and we brush the compliment aside because we are thinking: "Oh, that's not true," or "You should see me at home," or "This old thing? It's my sister's," or "I got it on sale," our self-talk reveals our limited perspective. We are not seeing beyond how we look "at home" and the fact that we got our dress "on sale"; we are not recognizing our eternal claim to a positive self-image. The worth we have outside of what we look like and what we are wearing eludes us, because we are focusing on the constraints of the here and now.

But if we graciously accept a compliment, we align ourselves with a godly perspective. Although we realize we are imperfect, we see ourselves as worthy of that (and all other) sincere gestures of praise because we have God-given worth—because we are God's children, endowed with the great gift of life. When we like ourselves not just because we look nice today but, more important, because we are children of God wearing the noble robes of royal birth, we make the divine connection to self-esteem. We think well of ourselves not just because someone complimented us but also because, by liking and respecting ourselves, we show more love and honor to Him who created us.

Self-effacing behavior is akin to what the Savior sadly described when He told of the third servant hiding his talent in the earth. Instead of capitalizing on what he *did* have, the servant was self-conscious and fearful about losing the talent he had already been given—not to speak of the *many more* talents his master might later have assigned to his stewardship. He lost what he had not just because he was afraid of losing it but also because he *hid* his talent. He lost his talent to the false security of the earth in which he buried it.

In the same way, we bury our talents every time we do not graciously accept a compliment or become gratefully aware of and honestly express the strengths we possess. This is not to say that we should put our strengths on parade and flaunt our talents, but it is to recommend that we be appropriately proud of what we have been given — even while we thank God for giving them to us. All of us have distinctive abilities, strengths and weaknesses, that cannot be exchanged for others' abilities but that can be developed in personalized ways. All of us have individualized blessings that we would probably not want to trade for others' opportunities. And all of us have unique trials and personalized problems. But in the words of an embroidered sampler that hangs on my wife's parent's wall, "If all of our troubles were hung on a line, you would take yours, and I would take mine" — and not just with regard to "troubles." It's probably true that if all of our blessings, abilities, talents, and even opportunities were hung on a line, "you would take yours, and I would take mine."

When a recognition of self-worth accompanies the development of our individual strengths, we will not be afraid of using and improving our talents because our worth will constantly fortify us. Our talents may fluctuate in the process of improvement, but our worth will not. One day we may seem more "gifted" than another, but as long as we are doing our personal best to discover and develop those gifts, our capabilities will manifest themselves and our sense of worth will fortify us. When the perspective of infinite worth defines our development, we do not think we are better than someone else as we discover our strengths, nor do we think less of ourselves when someone else seems to possess a talent we lack. Internalizing the belief that "no one is *better* than ourselves" and, on the flip side, "we are *no better* than anyone else" will lead us to the personal best that we are all meant to achieve. We can neither belittle nor boast about our strengths as long as we look to God as the giver of all gifts and the source of our worth.

S.A.C.K.

When we make a consistent effort to avoid the "gunny-sacking" of negative feelings and inadequacies, we fill our mental, emotional, and spiritual "sacks" with discovered talents and positive reinforcements. Or we:

> S = *Strengthen* ourselves by
> A = *Acknowledging* our worth,
> C = *Counting* our blessings, and
> K = *Keeping* our talents in good repair.

We can S.A.C.K. (strengthen, acknowledge, count, and keep) an attitude of gratitude. Because even if our mental, emotional, or spiritual sack is only partially filled, even if many of our talents remain "hidden," gunny-sacking will reveal a half-*empty* sack, while "S.A.C.K.ing" will disclose a half-*full* one. And while gunny-sacking feeds on inabilities and even disadvantages, "S.A.C.K.ing" concerns itself with strengths (or talents) and concentrates on abilities — discovered or undiscovered though they may be. Taking time to discover and develop the unique gifts God has given us will make our lives more full—and more meaningful. Our personal "bag of tricks" or "S.A.C.K. of talents," when stuffed full of all the good things with which we have been endowed, is an individual reminder of our inherent worth. God loves us so much that He gave us a unique combination of blessings, talents, and abilities that will enable us to achieve our personal best and that can also help to sustain us when we are at our personal worst.

Follow Your Bliss

Capitalizing on our talents in this way will fill our lives with a greater degree of happiness and a more accurate understanding of our potential. When we are pursuing those niches of personal performance that bring us the most joy, each day can become the first day of the *best* of our lives. The distinguished scholar Joseph Campbell encouraged his students to search out their talents by reflecting on the happiest moments of their lives. He advised: "The way to find out about your happiness is to keep your mind on those moments when you feel most happy, when you really are happy—not excited, not just thrilled, but deeply happy. This requires a little bit of self-analysis. What is it that makes you happy? Stay with it, no matter what people tell you. This is what I call 'following your bliss.' "[2] The fear of failure sometimes keeps us not only from following that bliss but also from recognizing what that bliss is. Sometimes we are so afraid not just of losing a talent but of even discovering it that we deny ourselves the joy of personal development. We stay in the melting pot of mediocrity and never really uncover our uniquely molded and divinely endowed strengths.

Henry David Thoreau tells of an alternate and more fulfilling approach to life. He says that one who "advances confidently in the direction of his dreams, . . . will meet with success unexpected in common hours." A recent study by author Srully Blotnick substantiates Thoreau's theory and proves Campbell's advice to "follow your bliss" to be sound—and even profitable. Blotnick and his associates studied a group of 1,500 people in their chosen professions over a twenty-year period. While most of the group emphasized money in their career choice, 17 percent chose a career in which they were genuinely interested. At the end of the twenty years, 101 individuals had become millionaires. And of those 101 people, all but one were from the 17 percent who "followed their bliss."[3] They had become successful in their professions because they were successful in discovering and then doing what they really enjoyed. They had found their personal best and worked to achieve it by designing a life, not just by making a living.

So how do we get the courage to follow our dreams? How do we acquire the confidence to search deeply inside ourselves and accept the combination of strengths and weaknesses that is uniquely ours? Certainly this is a difficult task to undertake by ourselves, on our own merits. But when we fully understand the message of several of the Savior's parables—and the premise of this book—we begin to tap the extraordinary power that quietly rests inside of us: the power of self-worth. From the prodigal son to the lost sheep to the lost coin to the parable of the talents, the Lord repeatedly reminds His disciples then and now that their worth (and every human being's worth) is great, even infinite and unchanging, in the sight of God. And this understanding is the key to unlocking the potential, the "best," that is latent within us. Only then do we realize our dreams.

Forgiving Ourselves

Even then, however, if we fail to forgive ourselves for the mistakes we have made, the fumbles and foibles that have hitherto prevented us from meeting with "success unexpected in quiet hours," we are equally neglectful. Paul bore witness to the Philippians hundreds of years ago that putting the past behind us and moving forward with faith is essential to our eternal progress. He declared: "I count not myself to have apprehended: but this one thing I do, *forgetting those things which are behind, and reaching forth unto those things which are before.*" (Philippians 3:13; italics added.) While Paul admits that he does not know all things, he does understand the need to "forget those things which are behind," to forgive ourselves for the things of which we have already been forgiven. He bears powerful testimony that before we can "[reach] forth unto those things which are before," we must put our mistake-filled past behind us.

To achieve our personal best, we must put those things that were not "our best" out of our lives — and out of our memories. Such a recognition of our self-worth requires an acceptance of the gospel of repentance and forgiveness (even of self-forgiveness). Scholar Hugh Nibley has summarized the gospel of Jesus Christ in two words: *repentance* and *forgiveness.* He says there are only two things we can do: (1) to repent and (2) to forgive. And he matter-of-factly suggests that we start doing them now! He makes the correct claim that those two processes are the irreplaceable concerns of any real Christian. In fact, a good measurement of the degree to which we have accepted the gospel of Christ and recognized our self-worth is the degree to which we can forgive ourselves for the failings of which we have already repented — to God and to others. Holding on to our "gunny sacks" of past mistakes and failures can be just as detrimental to realizing our personal best as the failure to recognize that we each have a divine endowment of talents.

Learning to Forgive Ourselves

The story of Bob McFarlane, a promising neurosurgeon who was following his bliss of medicine, offers some valuable insights into the subject of self-forgiveness. During his residency, this dedicated doctor started using injected opiates to relax his overworked nerves. Before long, he became addicted to the narcotics and was debilitated by his dependency. He was expelled from his residency and fell into a pattern of finding and losing jobs. For over a decade, he struggled to put his life back together: sometimes trying to cure his addiction by himself and sometimes going in for professional treatment. After entering a long-term chemical dependency program, he finally started to make some real progress. And he attributes this long-sought-after success to jumping the hurdle of self-forgiveness. He reflects: "My first hurdle was the overwhelming sense of shame and guilt at what I had done and the depths to which I had sunk.

Two little phrases that I learned there aided in my deliverance from the bondage of guilt: 'He retaineth not His anger for ever, because he delighteth in mercy.' (Micah 7:18) and 'God has absolutely no attitude of condemnation toward man.' Armed with these I could now set about learning to forgive myself."[4]

Faith in God was crucial to McFarlane's forgiving himself — and to his recovery. Because belief in God eventually translates into belief in oneself, McFarlane was finally able to find the power to beat his dependence. And now he helps many others do the same. After traveling the long road to recovery, Bob McFarlane returned to the medical profession as a specialist in chemical dependency and a committed consultant to the Drug Enforcement Administration.

Letting Go of Bananas

Sometimes the only thing between ourselves and our personal best is the lack of self-forgiveness. We, like the captured monkey, cannot let go of the "bananas" in our lives. Did you know that monkeys can be caught by putting bananas inside a trap? The monkeys put their paws inside the trap to get the bananas and do not realize that they cannot be freed unless they let go of the fruit. The monkeys try everything to get away. They try to pull the traps with them and even attempt to chew an opening through the metal. But they refuse to let go of their delicious prize. And eventually, despite a lot of effort and more than enough noise, the monkeys are captured without much trouble.

We have a lot more reasoning power than monkeys,

and yet we may still refuse to forgive ourselves for the times we have slipped on our own banana peels. All too often, we hold fast to the "bananas" of guilt, revenge, resentment, hate, and envy that feed a poor self-esteem and keep us from recognizing our self-worth. One of the most empowering understandings of godly improvement is that we are all changing, fallible people who are in need of repentance and forgiveness. We have all made mistakes. We have all failed at one thing or another. But we must realize that we are not our failures; just as we are not our mistakes or our mental and physical surroundings. We are worth more to our Father in Heaven than all the mistakes we have made (and will yet make). Because we are greater than our failures, we can always achieve greater personal successes than we are currently enjoying.

That is exactly what the now famous Colonel Sanders believed when, at the age of sixty-five, he embarked on what would be two years, thousands of miles, and more than one thousand unsuccessful attempts to sell his chicken recipe to restaurants across the country. Not satisfied with his $99 Social Security check and what he thought would be an uneventful life of a retired laborer, he decided to make the most of his later years by marketing his chicken recipe to any and all interested restaurant owners. Sleeping in the back of his car and traveling from one end of the nation to the other, he faced rejection over and over again until, on the one-thousand-and-tenth attempt, a restaurant owner decided to try it out and pay him a portion of the profit. As we all know, the rest is history. With a Colonel Sanders Kentucky Fried Chicken restaurant in almost every city in the United States, we have visible evidence of the power that comes from separating ourselves and our identity from our setbacks and failures — and from believing in our dreams enough to take action and fulfill our personal visions. Colonel Sanders knew that he was a person with worth and that his failures were only *events* in his life. And with that self-awareness, he was able to pick himself up time and time again until a restaurant finally accepted his recipe.

Believing in Ourselves

Just as Colonel Sanders achieved his personal best by putting his failures behind him and going forward with the faith that someone would eventually want his tasty chicken, so can all of us achieve our greatest potential by believing in our strengths and by not being discouraged or consumed by our failures. Thomas Edison conducted more than 10,000 experiments before inventing the incandescent lamp, but he learned from his "failures." In fact, he described the events prior to his breakthrough as "10,000 discoveries of how electricity did *not* work." He turned his failures into discoveries because he learned from his mistakes. He did not condemn himself for not doing things right the first time.

We may never concoct a winning chicken recipe, and the incandescent lamp certainly cannot be rediscovered, but all of us have defeated odds in some way or another and achieved our personal best. I think of a woman I observed while attending college. She went from one class to another in a wheelchair, barely able to move her hands and having no mobility in her arms and legs. I watched as she received not just a bachelor's degree but also a graduate degree in her field of study. For me, she was an unsung hero, a quiet achiever who did all in her power to achieve her personal best. And certainly her story is not isolated. I am well acquainted with a young single mother who is doing her best to raise four children alone. I am awed by her strength and patience, her miraculous resiliency in the face of serious challenges. Her commitment to care for and love her family—even while she is struggling to work and finish school—is truly remarkable. We see such wonderful accomplishments all around us. But do we ever stop to encourage others, let alone to pat ourselves on the back, for reaching a personal best? If not, we can start today.

I know a young man who practices the piano regularly, and after he plays a song without making too many errors, he stops his playing and claps for himself! This youth seems to have realized a life-enhancing truth: sometimes no one else may be applauding our efforts, and at such moments it is important to stop and "clap for ourselves," to recognize our efforts by rewarding ourselves in some way. Maybe your reward will take the form of a refreshing walk, a cold glass of water, or a fresh bouquet of flowers for yourself to enjoy; it does not matter what we do to encourage ourselves on our worth-guided road for improvement, but it does matter that we stop to recognize both the achievers around us as well as the personal achievements within us: those developed strengths in ourselves and in others that reflect best efforts.

God has given each of us specific and uniquely defined strengths to aid in our personal development. While we may seem to have more talents or fewer talents than others, and while those talents may go through different stages of development, we all have equal and unchanging worth. And we all have the promise of a glorious reward: immortality and eternal life.

SECTION 4

. . . .

TURNING OUTWARD

We are all worthy of God's love.
This realization leads to a greater acceptance,
appreciation, empathy, and love for others.

. . . .

CHAPTER 10

OUR JUDICIAL ROBES

How far you go in life depends on your being tender with
the young, compassionate with the aged, sympathetic
with the striving, and tolerant of the meek and the strong.
Because someday in life you will have been all of these.
— George Washington Carver

The divine connection to interpersonal success becomes
significantly more meaningful — even possible — when we realize that not only do we as individuals have God-given
worth, but that every other human being also has infinite
and unchanging worth. Acknowledging and respecting others' self-worth allows us to appreciate diversity, stay open
to uniquenesses, avoid crippling judgments, and believe in
others' abilities. Just as the internalization of our own worth
empowers us to turn personal goals and dreams into realities,
the deep recognition of *all* people's worth is an interpersonal
enabler: the key to unlocking the door of a more universal
success.

So what does it mean to acknowledge another's worth?
What kind of behavior manifests such an acknowledgment?
The Savior answers such questions when He concludes His
Sermon on the Mount (the greatest discourse on interper-

sonal relations). After having delineated the desirable attributes of a truly righteous and well-adjusted person, He
concisely summarized: "Judge not, that ye be not judged."
(See Matthew 5–6; 7:1.) Then he continued to teach with
some penetrating questions: "Why beholdest thou the mote
that is in thy brother's eye, but considerest not the beam
that is in thine own eye? Or how wilt thou say to thy brother,
Let me pull out the mote out of thine eye; and, behold, a
beam is in thine own eye?" (Matthew 7:3–4.) *The* Judge,
the One who has all rights and responsibilities for judgment
as our intercessor with the Father, finished His remarks on
righteous living by counseling His followers not to judge —
or not to form an opinion when their vision was clouded
by the motes of mortality and the beams of their own mis-
behavior.

Mote-Beam Disease

Some have called this kind of judgment the "mote-beam
disease," or the malady of misperceptions. It manifests itself
in most of the minor as well as many of the major problems
we confront. The mote-beam disease may inflict a nation, a
neighborhood, a company, a family, or a marriage. Many
of the problems between couples are found in such mutual
misperception. Perhaps a husband sees only the things his
wife does wrong: she is late for an appointment, she mis-
calculates the checkbook, the children are unkempt, or the
house is less than presentable. And maybe the wife concentrates only on what her husband is not doing: he does
not come home on time, he neglects certain chores, he
doesn't pay enough attention to her and to the children,

and he doesn't share the household duties. While each spouse concentrates on the things the other is doing wrong and forgets his or her own failings, he or she may lose sight of all of the other things that are going well for the couple: the promises that *are* kept, the chores that are done, the compromises that are achieved. Perhaps the greatest danger of such motes and beams is that the "real" picture becomes so distorted in the process of continually "picking apart" and finding fault that the original beauty of the relationship may be damaged — or even lost.

Similarly, many of the skirmishes between countries are rooted in such hypocritical judgments. One nation expects another to meet certain demands and make particular promises that the other nation is not prepared to make. Or even when that nation is meeting those demands and fulfilling those promises, it sometimes measures the other's expected output by its own input — or its own training, resources, history, people, and problems. In the process, both nations become more concerned about the actual "balance of trade" than a peaceful solution to the problems.

The same scenario often characterizes our neighborhoods. One side of the block expects the other side to be its clone: to have its standards, interests, and life-styles. And whenever one side defies the other's expectations, that side may make damaging judgments against the other by concentrating on the motes in neighboring houses and missing the beams that bar its own windows. When we perceive the world only through our own prejudices and expectations, we will never really see the warm hearth that may burn deep inside our neighbors' homes. But when we have been

in their homes and looked through their windows, we can
begin to understand why they have built their house — and
all that it holds — in the way they have. Only then can we
begin to comprehend their dwelling place.

The same principle applies to the interpersonal exchanges within those neighborhoods and homes, within an
office or in the marketplace: between the people themselves.
If we prescribe a life-style, an action or a reaction, or even
a certain appearance that is based exclusively upon our own
experiences and judgments, we are spreading the "mote-
beam" disease. But when our perceptive prescriptions are
restricted to our own behavior and beliefs — and not to the
behavior and beliefs of those around us — we begin to treat
the malady of misperception that plagues our society by
curing the cancers within our own souls. The healing process
is bound to be slow and will sometimes even involve sec-
ondary infections, but if we can begin to diagnose the problems of perception in our own person, we will make great
breakthroughs to achieving a more universal cure.

C. S. Lewis explained the danger of this interpersonal
disease of making false judgments:

> What can you ever really know of other people's
> souls — of their temptations, their opportunities, their
> struggles? *One* soul in the whole creation we do know:
> and it is the only one whose fate is placed in our hands.
> Because there is a God, you are, in a sense, alone with
> Him. You cannot put Him off with speculations about
> your next door neighbours or memories of what you have
> read in books.[1]

When we *assume* that we know why other people do

what they do and say, we may put ourselves between them and the most accurate and loving kind of judgment. Because we are ultimately "alone with God," we need to let other people be "alone with God," and one of the best ways we can do that is to appreciate diversity and love people for who they uniquely and individually are.

Strength in Diversity

If, in our relationships with our spouses, our children, our friends, and even with the strangers in our lives, we can appreciate differences and be strengthened by diversity, we will stop wasting our own prescriptive medicine on those who have different situations and problems than we do. We all have unique strengths and weaknesses. And because of that, our interpersonal sensitivities, reactions, and requirements will always be different from everyone else's — even from those who are closest to us.

With this recognition and with the realization of our infinite and inherent worth, we can more effectively interact with the people around us. When we begin to look at a spouse's difference of opinion not as a threat to our own way of thinking but as the means for together coming to a more expansive, informed, even inspired understanding, differences will strengthen — rather than put wedges into — our relationship. In a marriage as well as in an office or in any other relationship, the synergy that results from open discussion of alternate viewpoints leads to better solutions and ideas than would be possible if everyone thought the same way. If we can teach our children that their unique set of rules is the best set of rules for them, and that their friends' different rules are their friends' business, we will better help them to recognize the opportunities that come from obedience and the strength that can be derived from diversity.

I know a woman who, for religious reasons, had been taught not to drink certain types of beverages. She grew up in an area and went to a high school, however, where everyone else her age participated in the sort of drinking from which she abstained. But because she felt strongly about her beliefs and because she did not insult or condemn her friends for their beliefs (she *was* their friend), her personal stand became a more public project of abstinence. Her friends would arrange beforehand for her special drinking diet, and they only invited her to those parties where they knew she would be comfortable. Because she did not judge them for their beliefs and behaviors, they did not ridicule her for choosing a different life-style. In fact, they supported her in living up to her standard and would have been disappointed if she had relented. They would not allow her to slip. There was real friendship and respect between them, unmarked by the motes of self-righteous judgment (from either side). Because of that mutual respect, this woman was strengthened by her friends who had different beliefs and alternate approaches to life.

Real synergy is created from diversity. The precious perspective that we are all one of a kind and that we all have unique abilities makes the whole of our society, office, neighborhood, and home greater than the sum of its individual parts.

Not only would the world be a less-than-interesting

place if we were all the same, but it would also be less efficient and enjoyable. Imagine associating with people who really were exactly like you: who talked the same, walked the same, dressed the same, and thought the same. It would be like listening to Tchaikovsky's 1812 Overture — or some other symphonic favorite — in which only French horns were playing. Because there would be no instruments of distinctive sizes, shapes, and sounds, the chords would not resonate as deeply, the harmonies would be less brilliant, and the range of sound would be much more limited.

Just as the strength of a symphonic composition is derived from the diversity of the instruments, real power and beauty come from bringing differences together. The balance of contrasts is what makes a rainbow so pleasing to the eye, a symphony so pleasing to the ear, and different foods so pleasing to the palate. Variety and contrast make for more pleasing presentations of everything from music to nature to food. The diversity of elements accounts for much of their beauty and power.

The same principle applies to all of us. If we were each given the same talents, if we all pursued the same interests, if we all possessed and cultivated the same strengths, we would not really need to rely upon one another — or even to work together. But because, as Paul taught, "there are diversities of gifts, but the same spirit," we need to realize that we are in this life together. (1 Corinthians 12:4.) We are all engaged in the process of living — not by ourselves, in a vacuum, but with other people who are both different from and similar to us. In A Christmas Carol, Charles Dickens suggested that we concentrate on our commonality, even while recognizing our differences. He advised us to look upon other people "as if they really were fellow passengers to the grave, and not another race of creatures, bound on other journeys."[2]

Because of the divine parentage that connects us, we have the blessing and the responsibility of being "fellow passengers," of respecting and appreciating the diversity that makes us each unique. As Henry Martyn Field has written, "There is no brotherhood of man without the fatherhood of God."

The Lord's Model

The blessing of a good friendship, brotherhood, or sisterhood, is based upon mutual respect and love. Having a perfect love and a complete understanding of the worth of *all* God's children, the Lord Himself was characterized as "a friend of publicans and sinners." (Matthew 11:19.) As One who knew the power of righteous judgment, of divine discernment, the Savior was quick to caution us not to put another's progress (as well as our own) at the mercy of limited and limiting discriminations. Certainly, He would have us choose our friends and associates wisely, but He would not want us to have exclusionary (or exclusive) circles of friends. As One who fully realizes the eternal worth of each of God's children, Christ affirms our worth by admonishing us not to underestimate the worthiness of any of His children through ill-founded or unrighteous judgments: judgments which often take the form of unfriendly, condescending, or unfair behavior.

Nevertheless, neither His life nor His teachings suggests

that we should walk around in a fantasy land, believing that *everyone* is honest, *all* causes are upright, *every* situation is safe, and *all* diversity is good. He knows better than we do that there are men and women who will "curse you," "despitefully use you and persecute you," "revile you," and "say all manner of evil against you falsely." (Matthew 5:44, 11.) He is aware that it is necessary to distinguish between right and wrong behavior, good and bad performance, moral and immoral conduct.

He knows that excessive "open-mindedness" can close our hearts and minds to simple faith and godly direction. The popular "anything goes" mentality lends itself to too much doubt, skepticism, and disbelief than is worthwhile. And in all of our apparent "open-mindedness," we end up closing ourselves off to the whisperings of our conscience. We sequester ourselves from much that is good and right in our efforts to separate ourselves from anything that makes another person, idea, or thing seem wrong. Paul taught the Philippians centuries ago, "Whatsoever things are true, whatsoever things are honest, whatsoever things are just, whatsoever things are pure, whatsoever things are lovely, whatsoever things are of good report, if there be any virtue, and if there be any praise, think on these things." (Philippians 4:8.) By so seeking after righteous ways and godly practices, we will truly allow the Lord's forgiving and accepting love to work in us.

Christ cautions us, "Beware of false prophets, which come to you in sheep's clothing, but inwardly they are ravening wolves." (Matthew 7:15.) And His disciple Paul admonishes us not to be "tossed to and fro, and carried about with every wind of doctrine, by the sleight of men, and cunning craftiness, whereby *they lie in wait to deceive."* (Ephesians 4:14; italics added.) And we might add, they who "lie in wait to harm, corrupt, destroy, and even selfishly charm." Christianity does not suggest that we believe ourselves out of reality, forgetting the basic distinctions between righteous and unrighteous behaviors and beliefs, or that we be "tossed to and fro, and carried about with every wind of doctrine" — all in the guise of love and acceptance. The Lord knew there would be people and causes that "lie in wait to deceive."

Discernment versus Judgment

While He wants us to *discern* between false prophets and true prophets, between those who despitefully use us and those who really care about us, between those who tell the truth and those who lie in wait to deceive, He commands us *not to judge.* So in our efforts to avoid judgment, we must remember that it is given to each of us to discern. We have all been blessed with a conscience, the Light of Christ. Neither the Savior nor His disciples would have us purposelessly subject ourselves to a "den of thieves."

As stewards, we are responsible for maintaining a discerning character and following our God-given conscience. Just because someone asks us to supply our credit-card number, or to deposit now, or to enroll today does not mean that we should do it. We all make daily decisions about what we should support, where we should buy, what we should avoid, and whom we can trust.

Such judgments are vital to our well-being. God, our

Father, would have us be discerning. And whether we are aware of it or not, we already are discerning — to one degree or another. Life requires us to be so. How many times have you altered a certain business transaction because of a feeling: you just were not sure if you could trust the company or its representative. Or while in school, did you ever drop one class to add another that just seemed to suit your purposes better? As a parent, have you ever steered your children to choose one video over another even when its rating suggested propriety? As a teenager have you ever had a distinct feeling to avoid a certain activity — not clearly understanding why?

We all make choices that reflect our innermost, principle-centered values. And just because we choose one mode of life over another, we do not need to condemn those who have chosen different approaches and life-styles. This does not mean we don't try to persuade others with longsuffering, gentleness, and love unfeigned. But we must also accept their right to make their own choices. We simply need to take inventory of our motives for making decisions and then make sure our own lives are in harmony with the righteous discernments we have made.

The way to acquire this attitude of discernment, rather than of judgment, is to realize the inherent worth of all of God's children. When we realize that people who are different from us are still members of our heavenly family (they are, in fact, our brothers and sisters), the "judgments" we make are softened by the recognition of their unchangeable worth. Judgment evolves into discernment when we make decisions based on the uplifting belief that, regardless of mistakes, misbehaviors, and even evil intentions, all people are *worthy* of God's love. When we make such a realization, no matter how dishonest or dirty or undesirable a person or situation may seem to us, we bless our own lives with positive thoughts and inspiring insights. Even though we discern their character or intentions, we do not deny them their God-given worth by passing damaging or unrighteous judgments on them.

The Power of Godly Love

I have always been touched by the words to a hymn, "Lord, I Would Follow Thee," by Susan Evans McCloud. Each verse expresses the power that a Godly love and acceptance has in influencing others' lives as well as in transforming our own:

> Savior, may I learn to love thee,
> Walk the path that thou hast shown,
> Pause to help and lift another,
> Finding strength beyond my own.
> Savior, may I learn to love thee —
> Lord, I would follow thee.
>
> Who am I to judge another
> When I walk imperfectly?
> In the quiet heart is hidden
> Sorrow that the eye can't see.
> Who am I to judge another?
> Lord, I would follow thee.
>
> Savior, may I love my brother
> As I know thou lovest me,
> Find in thee my strength, my beacon,
> For thy servant I would be.

> Savior, may I love my brother —
> Lord, I would follow thee.[3]

Our discussion of judgment could be summarized in the simple but penetrating question of this song: "Who am I to judge another/When I walk imperfectly?" And our suggestions for avoiding judgment are captured in its final plea for divine assistance: "Savior, may I love my brother/As I know thou lovest me." A Christ-like love, based on an inherent and unconditional worth, is the catalyst for turning a self-centered judgment into a conscience-centered discernment.

This paradigm-shift from judgment to discernment is not an easy process. We all know that it can be difficult to distinguish between good and bad options, let alone between good and better choices. But when we begin to let the pure love of Christ, or charity, guide our choices, we will progressively move away from judgment and rely more wholly upon discernment. When we are motivated by understanding and love, we are inspired to make more righteous evaluations.

The Les Story

As the second half of the Savior's admonition (". . . that ye be not judged") implies, the avoidance of judgments is as beneficial to us as to those we might misread. I learned this valuable lesson a long time ago, after several years of misperceiving an acquaintance who is now a dear friend. I first met Les during my college days. I used to see him everywhere (and I mean everywhere) I went. He would be at the student center the same times I was there. He had classes in the fine arts building just when I had classes. I would see him in the bookstore almost every time I went to get supplies. And, it seemed, I never went to a party at which he did not make a grand appearance.

I never actually met him. I just noticed him — a lot. He was always surrounded by women, always talking, always standing taller than everyone else, and somehow always irritating me. I did not know his name until several months after first noticing him, and even then I found out through another person.

Shortly after graduation, I applied for a job in the surrounding community. After years of observing but never really knowing this person, I was not surprised to find that Les was applying for the same job. So there we were, both of us really not knowing each other, neither of us very relaxed, and one of us talking far more than the other of us wanted. The more Mr. Talkative carried on, the more I thought to myself: "He is really bothering me. I wish he would just be quiet. I am trying to mentally prepare for an important interview." But the chatter did not stop until we were both called into our respective interviews at, of course, the very same time.

After the interview, I made a quick getaway and thought that I would not be seeing this Les character again. But sure enough, on my first day of work, Les was there. We had both been hired. I do not remember much about my first days on the job, but I vividly remember sitting across from him in meetings, watching him talk, observing his animated gestures, and wondering how long I could cope with his nonstop "sociability."

I never did get away from him. After several months of interactions at work (and now years of association outside of work), I am most thankful that I had as many chances as were given me to get to know a man whom I now consider a true and trusted friend. I discovered a warm, gentle, and truly caring individual in Les. And while I then thought that *he* had changed since our initial exchanges on campus, I now realize that I was the one who had changed. I was the one who had been blinded by false perceptions and unfair judgments.

Les was the same person I first saw on campus several years ago, but somehow I was a different person for having become better acquainted with him. I had changed. Les had always been a great person with an accepting heart and an abundant attitude, but I had misperceived him. Once I put my "judicial robes" aside and embraced him with the nondiscriminatory garb of real friendship, I began to see Les for the good friend and loyal confidant I now know him to be. And we have since enjoyed an enriching and enduring friendship.

Taking Off Our Judicial Robes

As we have all done at some point in our development, I set myself up as an all-knowing judge of someone's character and was so wrapped up in the judicial robes of my own experience and limited understanding that I failed to discern a sincere and loving heart—a real friend who genuinely cared about my well-being. Fortunately, life is a process of maturation and growth. I learned a lot from my initial rejection of Les many years ago—as I am sure all of us have learned from similar experiences. In large measure, I was transformed by this extended encounter, and my life has been blessed with so many friendships and meaningful relationships as I have developed more accepting attitudes — as I have tried to avoid judgment and look into the hearts and souls of other people. I will ever be grateful that I was "forced" into cultivating what initially was an undesirable association, because I not only discovered the real Les, but, just as important, I unlocked a fundamental door to interpersonal success: not wearing judicial robes.

This "wearing of judicial robes" can be a humorously effective image to help us understand what we do to ourselves and others when we participate in inappropriate and unrighteous judgments. Imagine yourself in long black robes, sporting an ornately curled and flawlessly powdered white wig, walking into a room and having the audience stand for you, bow for you, and quiet down for you — and then see you trip on the very robes you wear so proudly. Most of us do not own, let alone wear, real judicial robes, but all of us have been metaphorically dressed in the distortionary robes of judgment. And all of us have tripped on those robes from time to time when our initial evaluation has been altered by the truth and hemmed with the measurement of true character. When we prescribe from our own autobiography, we are bound to stumble over our own definitions of how things should be (or *seem* to be) and into the revelatory reality of how things really are.

But when we base our interpersonal relationships on the belief that each one of us has equal worth in the sight of God, we will more readily and sincerely refrain from judging.

We all operate under different sets of expectations and different combinations of opportunities, but because we have an abiding worth that runs deeper than any and all of the circumstances and descriptions that characterize us, we have neither the right nor the responsibility to judge unrighteously. We are under God's stewardship, and He is the rightful owner of all judicial robes.

The Gentle Power of Empathy

By realizing our own and respecting others' self-worth, we replace judgment and discrimination with empathy and love. Empathy is the demonstration of Christ-like love. Or, as Denis Waitley so aptly said, empathy is "the recognition that each human being on earth is a person with equal rights to fulfill his or her own potential in life. It is understanding that skin color, birthplace, sex, financial status, religion, intelligence, and political beliefs are not measures of worth or worthiness."[4] Because our self-worth is an immeasurable source of strength and comfort, we all have the right — and the ability — to enjoy the warmth of empathy and to shun the frigidity of cold, harsh judgment.

Aesop told an enlightening fable about this principle. The wind and the sun had an argument about which one of them was stronger. They decided to test their strength on a traveler coming down the road. The one who could get the traveler to take off his coat the fastest would win the contest. The wind tried first, blowing with all his might, but the more the wind blew, the tighter the traveler drew his coat around him. Then the sun took a turn, warming him with his light. Soon the traveler removed his coat.

Warmth and gentle persuasion are always stronger than fear and force. And when we practice such warmth and gentleness, we show our empathy for others. Empathy is a powerful influence in helping others to change for the better.

When we have empathy for others, we try not just to understand but also to feel what they are feeling. We can have such empathy when we see their God-given potential as we see our own. By showing empathy, we demonstrate the eternal worth of ourselves and others, and we communicate love, which is the message we all need most.

Although we differ in many ways, we still share a common bond — we are all children of God. And no matter what our differences, we all have many more similarities: doubt, fear, and discouragement; faith, hope, and courage.

We can empathize with others when we understand our similarities. We can put aside our negative assumptions and unnecessary judgments, for God Himself finds us all worthy of His love. As Jesus said, "This is my commandment, That ye love one another, as I have loved you." (John 15:12.)

As God has loved us, let us love one another, looking for the spark of divinity that burns in the hearts of all people, the seed of godhood that may grow and bear fruit as it is nourished in love. As the oak grows from the acorn and the butterfly from the caterpillar, so may we grow in our Father's love and in the love and empathy of one another.

I will always be grateful for an experience I had while traveling that taught me the importance of empathy's gentle touch. After spending nearly twenty-five hours on several airplanes, I arrived in another country on a Sunday morning. To say I was exhausted would be an understatement. My clothes felt dirty, my face was unshaven, and my luggage was lost. But it was Sunday, and I wanted to attend church before embarking on what would be even more of a work-weary week. I found a church in the area, and because I did not have a change of clothes, I wore what I had traveled in — a sweatshirt and some wrinkled pants. The people at the service had every reason to look at my apparel and wonder why I was not dressed appropriately (they were all in suits and ties and dresses), but none of them did. They welcomed this American with open arms, showed me around the building, invited me to come back whenever I was in town — several even invited me over for dinner. They may have been wearing their Sunday best, but they certainly were not wearing their judicial robes. And because of their warm acceptance, I was more readily able to feel God's love during the worship service.

What Is Essential

In Antoine de Saint-Exupéry's timeless tale *The Little Prince,* the fox teaches an insightful lesson. After traveling the universe, the little prince encounters interesting characters from whom he learns much. But he learns the most profound secret from a fox. The wise fox divulges: "And now here is my secret, a very simple secret: It is only with the heart that one can see rightly; what is essential is invisible to the eye."[5] Herein lies a cornerstone for interpersonal success: seeing beyond the visible and into the hearts of the people with whom we interact. What is essential about ourselves as well as our associates is the invisible reservoir of worth that is our birthright.

This well-spring of worth is accessed through a Christ-like love, or an empathetic attitude. So we could say that what is essential for our interpersonal development is LOVE. Or,

> L = *Looking* for the good and
> O = *Overlooking* the bad by
> V = *Valuing* each other's worth and
> E = *Empathizing,* or putting ourselves in
>   each other's situations, "walking
>   in another's shoes."

Having a loving attitude means that we avoid unrighteous judgments by recognizing the divinely endowed worth in other people. And how do we demonstrate such a recognition? By looking for their innate goodness and overlooking some of the human foibles that (to varying degrees) characterize us all. When we approach our family, friends, and associates in the spirit of love and acceptance rather than of judgment and condemnation, we are better able to understand from where they are coming. We are better able to see all of the great and noble places they could be going. We are better able to love them as the Lord loves us.

We are able to empathize — and not just sympathize — with them. Sympathy has its place in human interaction. We all have moments when we need to commiserate, or as Webster defines it, "to be in keeping, accord, or harmony" with another person. But even commiseration falls short of understanding, or real empathy, which Webster defines as "vicariously experiencing the feelings, thoughts, and experience of another." We can have sympathy and not understand. But we cannot have empathy without really valuing the feelings and comprehending the worth of other people.

Christ's life is a perfect model of this empowering principle. Love brought Him into the world; love was the essence of His life and teachings; and love was the motivation for His redeeming sacrifice. John records: "God so loved the world, that he gave his only begotten Son, that whosoever believeth in him should not perish, but have everlasting life. *For God sent not his Son into the world to condemn the world; but that the world through him might be saved.*" (John 3:16–17; italics added.) And because Christ is our Exemplar, the same purpose applies to us all: God sent not each of us into the world to *condemn* the world, but to make the world a better place, a place filled with an empowering and motivating love, by exhibiting Christlike empathy.

The Power of Love

Our need for such selfless, even divine, love manifests itself in the interactions we have with our family members: those with whom we associate daily. It is much easier to love and accept someone with whom we have only passing exchanges and infrequent conversations, but it requires an entirely deeper and different sort of understanding and affection to satisfy the daily requirements for love in our own family. Referring specifically to the marriage bond but also describing a more general love, President Spencer W. Kimball explains:

> Love is like a flower, and like the body, it needs constant feeding. The mortal body would soon be emaciated and die if there were not frequent feedings. The tender flower

would wither and die without food and water. And so love, also, cannot be expected to last forever unless it is continually fed with portions of love, the manifestation of esteem and admiration, the expressions of gratitude, and the consideration of unselfishness.[6]

This flower metaphor became instructive and poignantly real for my wife and me when, early in our courtship, we planted some tulips together. The flowers became "love blossoms" of sorts, and as we worked together to nurture these perennial buds, we discussed the importance of understanding each other's daily needs for love and acceptance. While one bud may need more sunlight and another require extra portions of water, so our needs — though different — could be met by looking beneath the surface and into each other's hearts. By empathizing, by being a nourishing light instead of a damaging judge, we could fertilize our relationship with the discerning warmth of love. We look forward to the annual rebirth of these spring blossoms, just as we daily anticipate a renewing of our eternal commitment to love and cherish one other.

Because empathy is antithetical to judgment, when we allow empathy (or Christ-like love) to direct our interpersonal vision, the motes that have previously marred our outlook will be replaced with more compassionate understanding. When we make the divine connection in our interpersonal relations, the beams that once barred our interpersonal progress will now decorate the portal by which we gain entry into each other's hearts and by which we

help each other to realize our full potential. Avoiding judgment and realizing that "what is essential *is* invisible to the
eye" allows us to see a world full of capable, changing people
who are worthy of our unconditional love, encouragement,
and forgiveness.

. . . .

CHAPTER 11

FORGIVE AND FORGET

I have learned that life is an adventure in forgiveness.
Nothing clutters the soul more than remorse, resentment,
recrimination. . . . Forgiveness is a gift we need to give
not only to others but to ourselves, freeing us from self-
punishment and enabling us to see a wider horizon in
life than is possible under circumstances of guilt or grudge.
— Norman Cousins

The avoidance of judgment is not enough to ensure interpersonal success. When feelings do get hurt, when judgments have been made, and when wrongs are committed,
we need to forgive — and to be forgiven. And we all know
how difficult the practice of forgiveness can be. It's hard.
Very hard. But the hurts we endure can be healed. No
matter how deep the cut and how sensitive the sore spot,
we can find the strength to forgive when we draw upon the
healing power of Jesus Christ — when we allow others to
change as we ourselves are changing.

The Divine Connection

Unconditionally forgiving and forgetting requires even
more inner strength and godly love than not passing judgment. It is one thing to quell our own negative thoughts,

but it is entirely another thing to not be hurt by the negative words, thoughts, and actions of others. While not passing judgment opens the door to good relations, forgiving and forgetting is the hinge around which all interpersonal progress revolves. For example, when we only suspect that a neighbor is throwing grass clippings on our side of the fence, it is easier to maintain a Christ-like attitude toward our neighbor than if we actually see him or her throw those clippings. If we only suspect the neighbor of wrongdoing but have no proof, we can do no more (nor no less) than withhold accusations. We can work toward good relations by refraining from judging. But in the second case, because we know a certain neighbor has offended us, we take our interpersonal skills to an even deeper level of understanding by forgiving those trespasses. We not only withhold judgment, but we also withhold resentment, revenge, and recrimination.

The degree to which we can forgive others and can forget the mistakes they make is a measure of our interpersonal maturity — a scale by which we can chart our progress. The more we allow others to change by forgetting their errors, their past shortcomings and offenses, the more fully we have acknowledged their infinite worth. The more we forgive, the better we demonstrate a recognition of our own and others' worth, and the easier it is to lose ourselves in the forgiveness of others. People who are forgiving are always more selfless. They have found their own and others' worth by losing themselves in building up other people. They have demonstrated an understanding of the unconditional claim all people have to a perfect Father's forgiveness, love, and understanding by being more forgiving, loving, and understanding themselves.

Because we are all children of God and beneficiaries of the atonement, we have equal rights to repentance and forgiveness. We have the undeniable ability to repent and the unequivocal responsibility to forgive — *and to forget.* Forgiving and forgetting are such essential components of the improvement process that neither we nor our associates can walk the difficult road of life — and experience real growth — without these redeeming precepts. As Henry Ward Beecher so aptly said, "I can forgive but I cannot forget is another way of saying I cannot forgive."

A Piece of String

The extent to which an unforgiving attitude can halt our progress is well illustrated in the story "A Piece of String" by Guy de Maupassant. The main character, Hauchecome, goes to the village one day and has an argument with the harness maker. That same day, one of the villagers reports a stolen purse, and the village rallies together to catch the thief. Hauchecome happens to be on his way back home about the time the crime is reported, and the harness maker (with whom he is at odds) happens to see him stop and pick something up along the roadside. The harness maker does not see that Hauchecome only picked up a piece of string and, already disgruntled by their previous dispute, goes to the authorities to report "the crime." The harness maker claims that he saw Hauchecome pick the purse up off the ground and take it. The police officials immediately go to Hauchecome's home and arrest him. He protests and even shows them the piece of string that he retrieved. But they refuse to believe him. They ridicule him for the claim he makes and send him to prison.

The next day, someone finds the purse, and Hauchecome is released. He becomes bitter over the false arrest and refuses to forgive his accusers. He dwells obsessively on his mistreatment, telling everyone he meets how he was falsely accused and humiliated. He thinks of little else, and, over time, he begins to neglect his work, his loved ones, and even his own health. His obsession with the injustice renders him seriously ill. Even with his dying breath, he utters, "A piece of string, a piece of string."

Just as the harness maker's unforgiving attitude colored his perception of Hauchecome's roadside bending, Hauchecome's anger and resentment penetrated the farthest reaches of his life and ultimately led to his physical and spiritual destruction.

Many of us have a "piece of string"—whether it be a thin strand or a rope-like weave—of which we refuse to let go. But even when we are right in our facts, we may be wrong in our attitudes. If "correctness" keeps us from forgiving others' wrongs, our own "rights" may evolve into even worse wrongdoings. President Gordon B. Hinckley captures this concept well:

> How difficult it is for any of us to forgive those who have injured us. We are all prone to brood on the evil done us. That brooding becomes as a gnawing and destructive canker. Is there a virtue more in need of application in our time than the virtue of forgiving and forgetting? There are those who would look upon this as

a sign of weakness. Is it? I submit that it takes neither strength nor intelligence to brood in anger over wrongs suffered, to go through life with a spirit of vindictiveness, to dissipate one's abilities in planning retribution. There is no peace in the nursing of a grudge. There is no happiness in living for the day when you can "get even."[1]

In all cases, the unforgiving attitude is potentially more harmful than the actual injustices. When we have been wronged, we can still go on with our lives — even if it is painful to do so. But when we refuse to forgive — whether forgiveness has been solicited or not — we invoke more pain and suffering on ourselves and ultimately become emotionally debilitated by our stubbornness. Often the wrongdoers do not even suffer. They may be totally unaware of the hurtful things they have done. Even when they know they have offended and are piqued with some guilt, their pain is usually not as damaging as the self-inflicted sores that come from the refusal to forgive. An unforgiving attitude is like a life-threatening cancer that eats away at our insides and affects other parts of our life and being. Only the Lord's redemptive surgery is strong enough to prevent such a disease.

The Letter A

Once removed, the sore spots we endure may well make us more sensitive, more aware of the cancerous condition that once plagued us — and that may afflict others. In the famous novelette *The Scarlet Letter*, Nathaniel Hawthorne demonstrates how the Puritan community suffers more than the convicted sinner because of its refusal to forgive. The community disallows Hester Prynn from putting the sin of adultery behind her by causing her to wear a scarlet A on her chest for as long as she lives. Even though Hester becomes a great asset to the community, a selfless nurse and a charitable doer of good deeds, the Puritanical culture insists on her wearing of the scarlet letter.

After several years, a few people in the community are so appreciative of Hester's services that the A no longer signifies adultery to them. It comes to mean everything from "able" to "angel" for these forgiving few: "The letter was the symbol of her calling. Such helpfulness was found in her, — so much power to do, and power to sympathize, — that many people refused to interpret the scarlet A by its original signification. They said that it meant Able; so strong was Hester Prynn, with a woman's strength." For the hand-ful of people who saw Hester's A as an emblem of all her good qualities, they found a real friend with an unprece-dented and nonjudgmental compassion. They found com-fort in the scarlet letter's promise of forgiveness, and they found solace in its representation of repentance: "The scarlet letter had the effect of the cross on a nun's bosom" for them.[2]

File Cabinets by the Dozen

We may no longer put scarlet letters on adulterers, but we all engage in a more subtle sort of condemnation when we refuse to forgive — by not forgetting others' grievances. Or when we keep "files" on all of the wrongs we have suffered or on all of the mistakes others have made. Human nature would have us keep file cabinets by the dozen. But no matter how badly we have been hurt, and no matter how much we have learned from mistakes (both ours and those of others), nothing good comes from unforgivingly keeping track of others' wrongs — whether they have been repented of or not.

When we keep a file of every mistake our parents make, a file for every malicious word a brother or sister speaks, a file for every unkind look from a co-worker, a file for jealous responses from friends, and a file for the selfish actions of a spouse, we only hurt ourselves. Our file cabinet becomes cumbersome and heavy, too stuffed and stretched with resentment and anger to allow for personal or interpersonal growth.

Letting Go of the Past

All too often we thwart our own progress by holding on to others' mistakes — mistakes for which they may have already repented. And we do not bless our lives, and the lives of our associates, with the healing balm of selfless forgetting. An acquaintance of mine, whom we will call Mike, recounted a boyhood experience in forgiveness that had evolved into a manly struggle to forget. When he was an impressionable young Boy Scout in his community troop, he had a Scoutmaster whom he loved, respected, and even idolized. He looked to this man as a mentor and held on to his loving words of wisdom and experience.

Then, suddenly, the Scoutmaster stopped coming to troop meetings, and the boys were told that a replacement would be called. Mike explained how empty and disappointed he felt — how slighted and forgotten. He wondered why his grown-up friend would abandon them, and he held on to the belief that the change would be only temporary. Surely their Scoutmaster would be back for the summer campout.

But almost as soon as he comforted himself with that thought, he was told that the Scoutmaster would not be back. He had been caught shoplifting. He had not adhered to the Scouting ideals, and he was no longer considered a good influence for the boys. Mike felt personally betrayed. In his boyish way, he had invested much belief in his Scout leader, and that trust had been defiled. His initial disappointment turned to anger and disgust. He could no longer trust his old friend, and he would not let himself love the new Scoutmaster in the same way.

Shortly thereafter, Mike and his family moved to another city, and he did not hear from his Scoutmaster for many years. Mike is now in his forties. He was reading the newspaper one day when he came across a short article announcing the appointment of his former Scoutmaster to a respected position in his church and community. Mike thought: "Since when have they been asking shoplifters to be prominent citizens? Don't they know he is a criminal?" He was angry, deeply disappointed, and convinced that the Scoutmaster had lied to the authorities about his past.

Then something happened inside of Mike, and he demonstrated what I would call real forgiveness. He looked back at the article, lifted the picture of his former Scoutmaster close to his face, and remembered the man he had loved and respected. He reminded himself of the man who had sometimes carried Mike's backpack in addition to his own when the trail was rough. Mike recalled the man who had always had time for another story before they put out the fire. He remembered the man who had laughed with him, cried with him, and even knelt beside him in prayer at the end of a long day. And he forgot about the man who had made a mistake during one weak moment a long time ago. The Scoutmaster had never asked this Scout for forgiveness. Maybe he had not even known that he had hurt Mike. Nevertheless, Mike forgave him. He replaced his resentment with positive remembrances of his boyhood leader, and he gloried in his Scoutmaster's newfound success by recalling the good times of years gone by.

An Eternal Reservoir of Worth

We all may not have the providence to forgive another by replacing the bad with the good. Many times we are hurt by people and circumstances in which we have difficulty finding *any* good. We may not know our offender as being anything but bad and doing anything more than hurtful things. In those cases, more than in others, it is necessary to draw upon the eternal reservoir of worth to which all of God's children are entitled.

It may be necessary to search faithfully and to energetically believe that such unpleasant people have good qualities deep within them, that those qualities will eventually be found, and, most of all, that those people do have a divine inheritance of worth. As Andrew Carnegie puts it, you may have to "mine for gold; you must literally move tons of dirt to find a single ounce of gold. . . . You do not look for the dirt—you look for the gold." Sometimes we have to remove a lot of protective covering. Sometimes we may even need to explore our own inner caverns of complacency. In all cases, we will be able to replace the bad with the good when we pause long enough to discover the wealth of possibility, the reservoir of worth, to which we all have claim.

Walter Anderson, the senior editor of *Parade* magazine, teaches us of the interpersonal power that comes from "digging for the gold." As a young boy, he was physically abused by his alcoholic father. At sixteen he was desperate to leave home, and he dropped out of school. The next year he joined the Marines and was sent to Vietnam.

His experience in the service, however, had a maturing effect on him, and he began to turn his life around. He finished school and learned how to write. Then came marriage and a career in journalism. Though he was overcoming his childhood in many ways, Walter Anderson still nursed the scars of his father's violence. He found it difficult to control his own temper and often did things he regretted. At those stressful moments, Anderson recalls, "I saw my father standing before me, his fists raised, his eyes narrowed in rage. I had inherited that rage. I suffered from it — even now, ten years after his death."

He realized that, for his own progression, he needed to forgive his father. And he started that difficult and painful task by remembering his father's good qualities. One such quality was courage. His father had fought in World War II and had served as a volunteer fireman. Anderson also reflected on how his father's parents had themselves been alcoholics and how his father had grown up in poverty. The more he learned about the nature of alcoholism, the more sympathetic he grew toward his father. He explains the process of forgiveness: "I found that the more I worked on forgiving my father, the easier it was to forgive myself. I didn't have to be angry. I didn't have to fight." Anderson was finally able to forgive his father when he repeatedly remembered the good qualities he possessed and no longer allowed himself to brood over and resent the bad. The more he understood his father's own wounds, the more he forgot his own scars, and the stronger his interpersonal muscles became.[3]

While we cannot control what another person might say or do, we can control how we respond to those thoughts, actions, and mistakes. We cannot undo another's wrong-doing. But we can keep from doing more wrong by refusing to equate the mistake with the person, by remembering that what someone does is separate from who that person really is. We may dislike the performance, but we can still like the performer.

When a "file" of mistakes keeps us from recognizing the worth of the person behind those mistakes (grievous though the mistakes may be) as well as prevents us from realizing our own worthiness and maintaining our own happiness, our filing system needs to be reorganized around a Christ-like, or a forgiving, love. And perhaps our files of the past need to be replaced with more hopeful files for the future. By holding on to a file of mistakes, we let others act upon us, and we refuse to take action ourselves. We are letting their mistakes and misbehaviors misdirect and even control our lives. Such unforgiving files destroy faith and ignore worth — in ourselves and in others.

Leave It Alone

In a classic address, "Balm of Gilead," Elder Boyd K. Packer told of a man he called John who was embittered by a doctor's mistake. When John's wife, Mary, was delivering their first child, John's doctor came from another house call just in time to ease the crisis of the baby's unsupervised birth. But some days later, the young mother died from the very infection that the doctor had been treating at the other home on the evening of the baby's birth. John was so embittered by the doctor's carelessness that his whole life was shattered by this devastating event. He could not forgive him; never could he forget the injustice wreaked upon him.

A wise religious leader came to John and counseled him to "leave it alone." He reminded John that there was nothing he could do to bring his beloved Mary back, and the best thing he could do for his child and himself would be to come back to church and fill their souls with the enabling power of God's love. Not until John was much older could he finally muster the strength and understanding to do this, to put aside his bitterness and forgive the overworked country doctor who was just trying to help as many people as he could under very unfavorable circumstances.

We all know that it is always easier to talk about forgiveness than to actually practice it, especially when — like John — we are victimized by another's mistake. From observing this and similar experiences, Elder Packer advised: "If you have festering sores, a grudge, some bitterness, disappointment, or jealousy, get hold of yourself. You may not be able to control things out there with others, but you can control things here, inside of you."[4] When the wedge of a wrongdoing gets between us and another person or group of people, we diminish our own as well as other people's happiness. We deny them their right to change, to grow, and to repent, and we do not acknowledge their ability to be forgiven—by ourselves and, more important, by God. When negative interactions keep us from recognizing the universal worth of God's children and the undeniable birthright to repentance and forgiveness, we stop the spiral of self-improvement (both ours and theirs).

The Casting of Stones

In the Savior's profound terms, we cast the first stone. When the scribes and Pharisees brought a woman "taken in adultery" to be judged of the Savior, He defeated both of their unrighteous purposes (to convict the woman and to catch Him disobeying the law of Moses) by first responding nonverbally: "Jesus stooped down, and with his finger wrote on the ground, as though he heard them not." (John 8:6.) By ignoring their rude remarks and minimalizing this public "hearing," He clearly demonstrated that the woman's sin did not keep Him from loving the sinner. Trying to maintain as much of the woman's dignity as was left to uphold, He lifted himself up and invited, "He that is without sin among you, let him first cast a stone at her." (V. 7.) "And again he stooped down, and wrote on the ground." (V. 8.) Still not acknowledging the Pharisees' unkind demands nor publicly addressing the adulterous woman, Christ gave us a model of sensitivity when "again he stooped down, and wrote on the ground." With such meaningful silence, He solved the problem and taught a timeless lesson in interpersonal relations.

He affirmed both the woman's unchanging worth and the accusers' eternal worth by placing a private grievance back in its rightful (personal) domain and demonstrating that only "he that is without sin among you" can incriminate a sinner or refuse to forgive a wrongdoer. Sometimes we find it easy to categorize ourselves as being "without sin." *Sin* is such a serious word that it seems to reach beyond our everyday, "mundane" wrongdoings. Many of us pride our-selves in having never done anything *really wrong*. But the Savior may well have said, "He who is without mistakes, failures, disappointments, *without the need to be forgiven*," cast the first stone. In other words, let only Him who does not need to be forgiven, Him who is truly without sin (in all of its "large" and "small" forms), exercise justice.

The crowd's response tells of the effectiveness of Christ's methods: "And they which heard it, being convicted *by their own conscience*, went out one by one, beginning at the eldest, even unto the last: and Jesus was left alone, and the woman standing in the midst." (V. 9; italics added.) He did not need to point His finger. He did not even need to determine the accusers' right (or lack thereof) to accuse. He simply put the problem back into the hands of those who created it, without embarrassing or mistreating them and even while showing compassion to them and to the victim of their unkindness.

Only when the accusers left did He speak directly to

the woman. And again, His words are a manifestation of the woman's (and of all humankind's) worth: "Woman, where are those thine accusers? hath no man condemned thee? . . . Neither do I condemn thee: go, and sin no more." (Vv. 10–11.) The Savior's response to sin is a model for us all. Even when we are the ones who have been sinned against, if we can love the sinner without loving the sin, if we can refrain from throwing the stones of self-righteousness by gossiping and labeling and making more accusations, our lives will be filled with the peace that the Savior demonstrated when He serenely "stooped down, and wrote on the ground."

While we are not told what happened to the woman taken in adultery, about where she went and what she later did, we can imagine the kind of impact this encounter must have made on her life from the experiences we have had when someone has loved us unconditionally and forgiven us for wrongs of which we may or may not have yet repented.

Transformational Forgiveness

One of my favorite stories is the poignant account of forgiveness in Victor Hugo's *Les Misérables*. The main character, Jean Valjean, steals some food for his hungry family in a moment of desperation and is thrown into prison and forced into almost twenty years of hard labor. This experience leaves him hardened and bitter, and though a bishop treats him well after his release, Jean "repays" his kindness by stealing the bishop's silver. It does not take long for the police to capture him, find him in possession of the bishop's silver, and haul him back to the bishop's home to confess

his thievery. With Jean Valjean fully expecting to be se-
verely punished and subjected to another even longer prison
term, the police bring him before the bishop, with the silver
in his hand. The bishop looks at the silver, smiles, and
treats the traitor like a friend. He explains to the police
that he gave the silver to Jean Valjean, and then he
dumbfounds the prisoner by "reminding" him that he forgot
to take the silver candlesticks as well. He says that they
were also intended for him. This act of forgiveness and
charity deeply moves Jean Valjean, melting away his bitterness and causing him to literally transform his life.

The Power of Forgiveness

For the woman taken in adultery, for Jean Valjean, and
for each of us, the power of forgiveness can work a mighty
change, even a transformation, not just in the life of "the
forgiven" but also for the Christ-like forgiver. A forgiving
attitude can dramatically change the way we look at other
people and the way we respond to all kinds of situations.
When we have a forgiving approach to life, we allow people
to change, we see the goodness around us and within us,
and we inspire others to become more godly. The effect is
cyclical: the more forgiving we are, the more others forgive
us, the more readily God forgives us, and the better we are
able to forgive ourselves. As the Lord says: "If ye forgive
men their trespasses, your heavenly Father will also forgive
you: but if ye forgive not men their trespasses, neither will
your Father forgive your trespasses." (Matthew 6:14–15.)
As with all of the precepts of interpersonal progress, we
cannot take the "personal" out of an interpersonal rela-

tionship. We cannot forgive others and be open to their development unless, as the Lord demonstrates, we ask God to "forgive us our debts, as we forgive our debtors." (Matthew 6:12.)

All too often we block our own progress by holding on to others' "debts" — "debts" for which the price may already have been paid. As a result, we incur unnecessary expenditures of judgment, anxiety, and worry in our own lives. Whenever we substitute a forgiving deposit for a condemning withdrawal in another person's emotional bank account (whether the "wrongdoer" has made reparative deposits or not), we risk our own emotional bankruptcy. And we diminish our ability to make meaningful deposits in our interpersonal relationships.

Not long ago a friend told me an enlightening story. He said that he had been walking through the grocery store with his mother when they ran into one of his mother's old friends. They stopped and talked to the woman for several minutes and then parted ways as they turned down separate aisles. As soon as the woman was out of hearing range, the man's mother turned to him and said, "You know, she had to get married."

The man stopped talking for a few minutes and thought about the implications of what his mother had said. Because he knew that the woman had been married to the same man for more than thirty years, had raised a fine family, and had long ago put her problems behind her, he was puzzled by his mother's comment. His mother still remembered the woman for a mistake that was more than three decades old. And by continuing to label the woman with this bygone incident, the man's mother was failing to let forgiveness follow its complete course. The woman's progress was not crippled by her mistake of years gone by, yet in some small but meaningful way, his mother's relationship with the woman was not as rewarding because of this unfavorable and unforgiving remembrance.

William Shakespeare alternately tells of the sweetness of a more positive or merciful remembrance:

> The quality of mercy is not strain'd.
> It droppeth as the gentle rain from heaven
> Upon the place beneath: it is twice blest:
> It blesseth him that gives and him that takes.[5]

And so it goes for all of the self-helps that relate to interpersonal progress. We cannot expect to get something out of a relationship that we are not putting into it. We cannot expect to be forgiven if we ourselves are not forgiving. And we cannot expect to be forgiving if we fill our souls with hate, regret, resentment, and revenge — if, like Hauchecome, we brood over the wrongs that have been wreaked upon us. But when we turn those feelings of injustice around and make the divine connection to improvement, we can constructively forgive.

We can lose our own grief to the relief and prevention of others' grief. When Candy Lightner's daughter was killed by a drunk driver in California, she decided to channel her heightened emotions into the founding of an organization that would fight drunk driving. Instead of succumbing to anger and pain, she rallied other mothers who had similarly been victimized and started what we now know as MADD

(Mothers Against Drunk Driving), a nonprofit organization that educates our nation on the risks of driving under the influence of alcohol. Subsidizing her efforts with an intricate telemarketing system and organizing presentations for school groups as well as programs for adult support groups, Candy turned her resentment into an empowering form of healing and forgiveness. She not only came to terms with her own grief, but she has also helped numerous others go through the same cathartic process.

Small Acts of Forgiveness

We can make such an attitudinal turn-around by not letting everyday opportunities for forgiveness pass us by. As ethereal as it may sound, it is possible to develop a forgiving attitude by first mastering our responses to the simple and sometimes subtle misbehaviors that we deal with all the time. When a toddler spills his cereal for the fifth time in one day; when a child forgets to take her lunch to school — again; when a teenager fails to call home before staying "just an hour later"; when a spouse loses your house key; when a co-worker calls you by the wrong name over and over again; when a friend forgets your birthday — if we can respond to such minor offenses with a gentle, sensitive reproof (immediately followed by an increase of love), we will more readily "turn the other cheek" when we are confronted with more damaging offenses. (See Matthew 5:39.) We will begin to make the careful balance between justice and mercy that the Savior exemplified when He told the adulteress, without condemning her, to "go, and sin no more." (John 8:11.)

But because we are not perfect and because our understanding is limited, because we do not have the same power of forgiveness and discernment as the Lord, the scriptures suggest that our interpersonal scale of justice and mercy should be weighted on the side of mercy.

THE BALANCING ACT OF FORGIVENESS

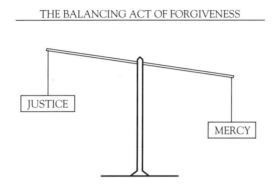

The Savior implored, "Be ye therefore merciful, as your Father also is merciful" and "Blessed are the merciful: for they shall obtain mercy." (Luke 6:36, Matthew 5:7.) But nowhere in the New Testament are we told to right all of our wrongs, take the law into our own hands, or have all of our grievances redressed. The Savior fulfills the law of Moses and no longer admonishes an "eye for an eye, and a tooth for a tooth." Instead He suggests that we turn the other cheek. (Matthew 5:38–39.) Otherwise, the whole world would end up blind and toothless!

Seventy Times Seven

We are commanded to unreservedly forgive. Peter posed a question to the Lord that most of us have probably asked at some time: "How oft shall my brother sin against me, and I forgive him? till seven times?" (Matthew 18:21.) We have all probably wondered when we can stop forgiving someone for a repeated offense. At certain moments, we would like to force retribution and forgiveness and write our own formula for justice. There have been moments when each of us has probably wanted to stop forgiving and forgetting, to stop turning the other cheek and "go for the throat."

But the Lord makes clear to Peter, and to all of us, that our responsibility is to be forgiving, and His calling as our Redeemer is to achieve the perfect balance between justice and mercy that we long for in this life but that we may not realize until the life to come. He responded to Peter's query, "I say not unto thee, Until seven times: but, Until seventy times seven." (Matthew 18:22.) When I read this scripture as a youth, I used to mischievously multiply seventy by seven and remind myself that I had to forgive someone only 490 times! I have since come to understand the saving implication of this counsel: we are to forgive without limit and without price. Because He paid the ransom for our sins, we will be alone with Him in determining the cost of our penance. No one else will ultimately determine when we have been forgiving or forgiven too mercifully or too many times.

Christ-like Forgiveness

As imperfect children, one way we can acknowledge the eternal worth of others is by sincerely forgiving. When we unconditionally forgive other people, we show them how much we believe in them, how fully we recognize their inherent worth and potential, and how completely we are willing to help them make changes for the better.

My father was a very forgiving person, even though as a child I did not fully appreciate his forgiving attitude. I remember a few occasions when his Christ-like attitude frustrated me. I wanted him to strike back, fight for his rights, cash in on his debtors, and get an eye for every injured eye, a tooth for every broken tooth. But he repeatedly forgave—and forgot. He demonstrated a Christ-like love and understanding that amazes me to this day.

I learned from his forgiving acceptance of others. Certainly not all of the time, but many times his mild manner would change the very tone of a conversation. His sincere smile would turn a situation around. And I would see countenances change and hearts confide. By loving others in spite of their differences, he reminded them of their God-given worth. His love bespoke God's love and touched a familiar place in my heart—as well as in the lives of many others. In his own humble way, my father had made the divine connection to interpersonal power.

We all can make such divine connections to better human relations when we practice the enabling principle of forgiveness. By relying on the redeeming power of the atonement and recognizing the universal worth of God's children, by forgiving, we put our human shortcomings aside and demonstrate a more divine understanding. We lose ourselves in the building of each other, and we ease our own suffering by relieving others' pain — or by having faith enough to forgive. A forgiving attitude is a believing attitude. And just as believing in ourselves is a prerequisite for personal progress, believing in others is essential to interpersonal success.

CHAPTER 12

BELIEVING IN OTHERS

> When we treat a man as he is, we make him worse than he is. When we treat him as if he already were what he potentially could be, we make him what he should be.
>
> — Goethe

God, our Father, has a perfect faith in each of us. He demonstrated this empowering trust by offering His Son as a sacrifice for our sins, giving us the individual opportunity for redemption and the personal responsibility for righteous living. By allowing us to choose between spiritual life and death and by giving us the means to repent and to be forgiven, He has already given us the assurance that we can return to Him. He has expressed a perfect belief in our ability to succeed while here on earth by virtue of His sending us here. And this belief is proof of the inherent worth we all possess. Because God believes in the worthiness of His children, in that very gesture of belief He endows us with an infinite and unchanging worth. His perfect faith is empowering in the truest sense. We are endowed with power and worth because He believes in us.

To a lesser degree, the same process takes place every time we believe in someone else. When we sincerely believe in the abilities of others, we help them to create these abilities. Conversely, when we doubt the capabilities of others, to some extent we prevent them from developing those capabilities. The Lord promised us that "all things are possible to him that believeth," not because we are all fully developed but because He has a perfect understanding of the power within us. (Mark 9:23.) Because our God-given and faith-inspired worth ultimately enables us to do "all things through Christ which strengtheneth [us]," the degree to which we recognize that worth and believe in its universal power determines how well we can help each other to do "all things." (Philippians 4:13.)

We Find What We Look For

Perhaps this rather intangible truth is more approachable from the pedestrian perspective of a country whittler. The story is told of an old man who sat in front of a country store, whittling away, not making anything in particular, just whittling, chewing on a blade of grass and occasionally sipping a glass of lemonade. One day a station wagon with an out-of-state license plate and a car full of furniture, bags, pets, and children pulled up. A middle-aged man got out of the car and asked the old man for directions to a neighboring city.

"Can you tell me how to get to the next town?" asked the driver.

"Sure can," answered the old man, not missing a beat with his knife and wood. "Yonder," he said, pointing with his pocketknife. "Down that road a piece."

"Thanks," said the driver. "Say, what are the people in the next town like?"

"What were the folks like in the town you just came from?" asked the old man.

"Not very friendly," said the driver. "Always thinking of themselves and how to get ahead. We were glad to get out of that place."

The old man nodded his head. "I think you'll find the folks in the next town are about the same."

Disappointed, the man got back into his car and drove down the road.

Not long thereafter, a second station wagon, also overloaded with furniture, bags, children, and pets, pulled up alongside the country store. A middle-aged man got out of the car and asked the old whittler, "Can you tell me how to get to the next town?"

The old man told him, and the second driver asked what the people in the next town were like.

"What were the folks like in the town you just came from?" responded the old man.

"Some of the best people we have ever met. Friendly, always willing to help you out. We're sure going to miss that place."

The old man nodded his head. "I think you'll find the folks in the next town are about the same."

Pleased, the driver got back into his car and drove in the direction of the "friendly" town.

The old whittler in this story seems to know one of the great truths of life and one of the keys to interpersonal success: we tend to find what we look for. Our mindset or orientation toward a certain place, situation, person, or group of people usually determines the nature of that place, situation, person, or group of people. We can literally create the kind of experience we will have with someone or something by the way we perceive and what we expect from that person or thing. The essence of our belief in large measure determines the nature of our reality. Our thoughts and attitudes formulate our own self-fulfilling prophecies.

What We Expect — We Find

I came to this understanding in my own life the first time I left for a business trip to Atlanta (and I have seen it in many other cities all over the world). I talked to several different people before I went, and they all told me how much they enjoyed Atlanta. They told me about the beautiful weather, the wonderful Southern people, and the fast-paced but friendly city. I was eager to enjoy the city for myself. And as might be expected, I found everything to match their description. I had a terrific time in Atlanta, and I continue to find it very pleasant every time I return.

Conversely, before another business trip in a different part of the country, I was told terrible things about the city I would visit. Several different people told me to watch out for the temperamental weather, the dirty streets, and the unfriendly people. I had conjured up an unpleasant image of the place before I actually saw it, and, as might be expected, that image was much like my perception once I arrived. I was told to watch out for all of the negative features of the city, and because I was on the alert for them, I discovered them. In retrospect, I am sure that I missed many of the wonderful people and things there. But I did find what I was "looking" for. (Of course, not every time someone has told us a place is undesirable do we find it so. Many times we find a location to be contrary to its description — positive or negative. But oftentimes, our expectations of a place paint our perception of that place.)

The same principle applies to our interpersonal relations. If we start a job expecting to dislike our new employer and to be uncomfortable with the other employees, we will most likely develop those negative feelings. If we believe that a spouse will be unpleasant and respond in a certain predictable way, our spouse will most likely react in just that way. If we think a child will make wrong choices, our disbelief in the child's ability to make good choices will certainly affect his or her decision-making. When we suspect that a friend will not be loyal, that friend may detect our distrust and feel less responsible for keeping up his or her end of the relationship. The degree to which we believe in others is perhaps the greatest determinant of how well we get along with others, how well others respond to us, and how much of an influence for good we are able to have in the lives of others.

Small Acts and Simple Words

This enabling belief in other people is most often demonstrated with small acts and simple words of praise. I remember the generous report a Sunday School teacher gave my mother one Sunday after church. She pulled Mom aside and said that I was such a delightful student, so good natured and so well prepared. She could always count on me to give the answer she wanted to hear. When my mother came home and told me what my teacher had said, I blushed with pride. I was only nine years old, but I remember it as vividly as if my mother had told me just this morning. The next Sunday when I went to class, I sat a little straighter in my chair, folded my arms a little tighter, and wanted to behave even better for my teacher. I knew that she believed in me, and I wanted to uphold — and even exceed — that belief.

The effects of heartfelt praise are far-reaching and long-lasting. We all have the need to be appreciated. When we try to improve, we need to know that our daily efforts to learn and grow (no matter how small they may be) are acknowledged by someone. We all need to know that we matter. Unfortunately, some of us may go for days without hearing a kind word, an encouraging comment, or even the faintest expression of approval from someone else. As any employee knows, we generally hear a lot more criticism from our bosses or co-workers than we do praise. Paul Thompson, the former dean of the BYU Marriott School of Management, said: "Managers should realize that many professionals who are deemed to be 'low potential' are not really low potential at all. Viewing or labeling employees as 'low potential' is a perception or practice that may create the reality. Thank goodness many employees considered to be low potential greatly outperform their labels."[1]

This trend toward destructive labeling and criticism seems to characterize our society. One study showed that the average parent-to-child criticism/compliment ratio is twelve to one. For every one instance of praise, there are twelve moments of criticism. And the numbers are even less encouraging in the classroom. On the average, teachers offer their students eighteen criticisms for every one compliment. While constructive feedback has its place, a critical attitude and approach to life is debilitating—for both the giver and the receiver. Children as well as adults usually live up (or down) to expectations, and constant criticism can convince them that greatness is out of their reach—as it is beyond your expectations.

It takes only a few seconds of time, even a few ounces of energy, to let someone know that he or she is appreciated. If we take special care to be on time, stop to ask "How are you?" pause to smile, give a hug, or express gratitude; in effect, we acknowledge another person's worth. We let others know that they are important to us—so important that we would stop what we are doing or put our plans on hold for them.

The Power of Praise

A highly decorated statesman, the Duke of Wellington, was asked late in life what he would have done differently if he could live his life over again. He did not say he would change the way he fought the magnificent Battle of Waterloo—or any other battle. He simply said, "I should have given more praise."[2] And many of us could probably say the same of our behavior. No matter how much praise we give to others now, we could all give even a little bit more. If we look for them, there are opportunities for praise all around us: in the first steps during rehabilitation, in the improved responsibility of a son or daughter, in the helpful assistance of a spouse, in the dedication of a co-worker.

Sincere praise, or the expression of a worth-inspired belief in others and in their abilities, can be a sustaining force for us throughout our lives. Words of praise and feelings of commendation are never forgotten. We hold on to such kind and uplifting words. Those expressions of encouragement fill reservoirs of praise that we — as well as our children, spouses, and friends — can draw upon for days, and even years, to come. They motivate us to give more praise, and they inspire us to live more praiseworthy lives.

In all of our efforts to offer praise, it is important that we not become flatterers. Flattery is insincere and excessive and may be prompted by ulterior motives. But praise by nature is not manipulative. It is motivated by the sincere desire to extend kindnesses and support. It is a deserved commendation, sincere expression, and heartfelt recognition.

For all of us who give and receive praise, let us not seek after "the praise of men more than the praise of God." (John 12:43.) The most meaningful praise we can receive is the peaceful assurance we get from doing what is right, from aligning our actions with our conscience and with an understanding of our divine worth. When we feel the soul satisfaction that comes from righteous living, we are the recipients of a perfect and completely selfless praise, praise from our Heavenly Father. And from this perfect model of praise, we are inspired to look for more opportunities to praise and to believe in each other's praiseworthiness.

Others' positive comments and believing attitudes enable us to perform at increased capacity. When I got a job as a TV news anchor in Pennsylvania, I was just out of my graduate program and a little nervous to be on the nightly news. I had to remind myself regularly that the news director and the general manager had gone to great lengths to get me to move to Pennsylvania. I knew they had a lot of confidence in my abilities, and I knew they had invested a lot of time and money in my position. Because my supervisors voiced their belief in my potential and demonstrated great confidence in me, I wanted to meet their level of expectation. And eventually I did. Now, when I look back at the video tapes of my first broadcasts, I smile at my rookie ways and critique my own beginnings. But I am grateful that my employers had enough foresight to see past my inexperience and believe in my broadcasting potential. In substantial part, they believed me into succeeding at my position.

The Power of Belief

The enabling power of belief has been chronicled through the ages: someone recognizes the worth of another human being and leads that person to discover his or her potential. The Greeks were so captivated by this idea that they related how Pygmalion, king of Cyprus, fell in love with an ivory statue of his own carving. His sincere affection and abiding love were so strong that Aphrodite, goddess of love, breathed life into the statue.

Modern playwrights and screenwriters have given contemporary interest to this ancient myth — and the abiding truth behind it. In My Fair Lady, for example, an uncultured woman grows into a picture of grace and beauty because Professor Higgins and his colleague believe in her. Eliza R. Dolittle learns to correctly speak, walk, dress, act, and even eat under their tutelage. And the street girl eventually passes

herself off as a duchess at a grand ball. The professor is strict
because he has high expectations for her; as a result, she
undergoes a delightful and endearing transformation.

Not only do we tend to find what we look for, but we
also tend to become what other people find in us. When
someone takes the time to acknowledge who we really are
and what our divine capabilities are, when someone makes
the divine connection for us — and helps us to make it for
ourselves, we can become transformed by their understanding of the greatness within us.

I am inspired by the story of a friend of mine, an outgoing
businessman who grew up on a farm in a small town in
Idaho. He describes himself as having been a shy, almost
backward youth who found security in the rigors of his chores
and solace in his animals' acceptance of him. He had difficulty speaking. His slight but noticeable stuttering often
made speech uncomfortable and sometimes embarrassing.
He would hurry home from school to spend time with his
barnyard friends, and he avoided most kinds of social interaction with his peers.

A speech teacher at school had taken notice of the boy,
observing him in the halls and in the lunch room for several
months. He wondered if the boy would ever find his way
into his classroom. But after several more months of only
passing hellos and what seemed to be one-way conversations, the teacher decided that if the boy was not going to
come to him for help, he would go to the boy — in his grain
fields, where he felt most at home. One crisp day in late
fall, when the harvest was over and the winter weather
seemed to be settling in, the teacher waved to the boy across

the partially plowed field. The boy stopped the tractor and walked over to his teacher, meeting him about midway. The teacher had a proposition for the student; he wanted him to enter the district speech competition. To do so, the boy would first have to win the school's tryouts. To say that the boy was shocked would be an understatement. He could not understand why the teacher would even consider him for such a competition. How could he address an auditorium full of people?

Several months and many tutoring sessions later, the boy not only competed in the district competition but he also won first place. The teacher had worked with him every day, sometimes all night long, inviting him home, feeding him dinner, meeting him at the school, and helping him practice at the podium until the stuttering was less and less noticeable — and then completely gone. They also spent many hours together writing the speech the boy would give. Encouraging but not overbearing, the teacher guided the boy to write something of which he would be proud. For a farm boy who loved the land, it was only natural for him to speak on the award-winning topic of soil preservation.

Who would have guessed that this quiet boy with a subtle speech impediment would not only win the competition but also become a proficient and heartwarming speaker? As an adult, the boy thanks his speech teacher for believing in him, for loving him enough to know that he had the ability to speak. The teacher had recognized the worth of this one shy student, and the student has gone on to help numerous others recognize their individual worth. In fact, "the worth of souls" is one of his favorite topics.

As a successful businessman, he spends most of his day speaking to other people and using the power of positive belief to motivate them to perform well—both on and off the job. He has become a mentor to many people, an example of the power of believing in others, because he (like his teacher) believes that all people have immense worth in the sight of God.

As with other worth-inspired precepts of interpersonal relations, the effects of believing in others are synergistic and rewardingly cyclical. The giver of encouragement is always a receiver. What goes around in our daily interactions truly does come around. The more we believe in others' divinely endowed worth, the more others seem to believe in us.

Charity Never Faileth

This undaunting belief in other people is what the Apostle Paul terms "the pure love of Christ," or charity. In his classic speech to the Corinthians, he describes a charitable person as one who "beareth all things, *believeth* all things, *hopeth* all things, endureth all things." (1 Corinthians 13:7; italics added.) And then he promises, "Charity never faileth: but whether there be prophecies, they shall fail; whether there be tongues, they shall cease; whether there be knowledge it shall vanish away." (V. 8.) But *charity*, or abiding love and belief, *never fails*. We may have all the facts and figures in the world, all the right equipment and all the necessary knowledge, but unless we have a resilient belief that withstands adversarial blows and overcomes even another's disbelief, if we "have not charity, it profiteth [us] nothing." (V. 3.) Only when we have charity and wholeheartedly believe in other people and in true principles, can we come to understand what really matters. We bless our lives with a recognition of God's perfect belief in us, and we empower others by sharing that godly belief.

We often see this interpersonal force at work in the relationships grandparents have with their grandchildren. Children often behave better for their grandparents than they do for their parents (and not just because their grandparents usually spoil them). Frank Morris in his book *Grandparent Wisdom* explains that grandparents often have higher expectations for their grandchildren than do their parents. And the children often live up to those higher expectations. Grandparents just expect the children to be polite, friendly, or quiet, whereas some parents seem to operate under the opposite expectations. Parents' perceptions may become so clouded by all of their children's daily demands and misbehaviors that they forget the sometimes less visible and certainly more meaningful attributes that those children possess as children of God.[3]

In other words, sometimes we may forget that our own children are first and foremost children of God, endowed with divine capabilities and inherent worth. Consequently, we may exhibit a less believing attitude toward them. Grandparents, however, may find it easier to believe in children's divine potential because they are usually a few steps removed from the children's day-to-day challenges and interactions.

The Abundant Mentality

Sometimes it is easier to understand what this grand-parental, even godlike, positive belief in others is like by ascertaining what it is *not* like. One of the most apparent indicators of a believing approach to life is a mentality of abundance rather than a mentality of scarcity.[4] When we rejoice in another's success, glory in another's victory, and cheer for another's accomplishment, we have what has been called an abundant approach to life. We are well enough grounded in our own worth that we do not need to feel threatened by another person's achievement and ability. But when another's success seems to diminish our own sense of accomplishment, we suffer from a scarcity mentality — or a lack of personal as well as interpersonal recognition of worth.

We may want others to do well but not *too* well. For example, we are happy for our friend's son as long as he is not competing against our own son. Or we are glad our neighbor bought a new car as long as we have a better car — or at least as long as our car is in good repair. And we glory in our co-workers' advancements insofar as they do not threaten our own position. As long as their success does not overshadow our own, we are glad to see them excelling. We look at success — and worth — as a scarce commodity that can be added to and subtracted from, not as the constant source of strength that it really is.

Of course, most of us probably fluctuate between an attitude of scarcity and an attitude of abundance. On some days we may exhibit both attitudes at different times. But working toward an abundant mindset is the challenge and opportunity of life.

You might evaluate your progress by determining where you (in general) and your actions (in particular) fit on the *scarcity/abundance* scale:

SCARCITY ◄——————————► ABUNDANCE

covetous ◄————————►	believing
jealous ◄————————►	forgiving
envious ◄————————►	accepting
judgmental ◄————————►	loving
resentful ◄————————►	empathetic

Surprised by Greatness

A good measure of where we stand on the scarcity/abundance scale is the degree to which we are surprised by greatness. Sometimes we tend to have such negative expectations of others that when someone really does do something commendable — when someone exceeds our expectations — we are shocked by their outstanding performance. We do not know how to congratulate them because we are so stunned that they could do something so congratulatory.

I have a friend who worked long and hard to become a heart surgeon. After studying diligently for many years in college and during medical school, and then working for six years as a resident, he finally entered the medical profession as a highly trained specialist. But when he goes home to visit friends and family, many of them undermine his achievements and treat him as the little boy he once was. They joke about his proficiency and, in subtle but hurtful

ways, demonstrate their disbelief in his professional exper-
tise. He hears remarks like, "I would never let the little
brat who broke my window operate on me!" "How could
a mischievous little boy grow up to be so successful?" and
"Who took his tests for him? There's no way the teenager
I knew could have passed such difficult exams."

But people change. We grow and develop. We learn
and live anew because there is power and potential within
us all. And whether that greatness manifests itself late or
early or in the middle of our lives, it has always been and
always will be there. As sculptor Henry Moore so aptly
wrote, "The sculpture is in the stone." There was nothing
he gave the stone that was not already contained within
it. The masterful sculpture had always been a part of the
rough stone he carved. But it took an imaginative and
believing eye to uncover that potential.

A Work of Art

So it is with each of us. There are masterpieces all around
us, waiting to be discovered, shaped, and admired. Within
each of us is a sculpture of greatness. As children of God,
we all have the raw material necessary to become a human
work of art—even as we help others to become their own
masterworks. The art of interpersonal relations is a function
of seeing the sculpture in all of the "stones" around us,
believing in the visible and invisible capabilities of our
friends, family, neighbors, and associates, as well as in the
grouches, grumps, and difficult people in our lives. When
we stop being surprised by greatness will we really see and
help others uncover their inherent talents and beauty. We

can become a worth-inspired sculptor who carves stones into sculpted wonders.

Pause to evaluate how much greatness you see in those around you. Would you be surprised if the little "bookworm" next door turns out to be a computer wizard and a multi-millionaire, writing innovative software programs to help the world? Would it shock you if the plain-looking teen who is not much of a babysitter inspires thousands with her practiced playing as a concert pianist? Or what about the woman at work who seems antisocial and never goes with her co-workers to lunch. Would you be surprised if she spends her lunch hours serving others at a homeless shelter? Or do you already look for these noble traits in your associates? Do you already see much of the greatness that resides in those around you?

These are important questions to consider. The degree to which the people in the time of Christ were surprised by greatness seemed to determine their acceptance of Him. When Christ announced His divine Sonship at His local synagogue in Nazareth, the people responded with disbelief. He finished reading several prophetic passages in the scriptures, closed the scroll, and said, "This day is this scripture fulfilled in your ears." (Luke 4:21.) Many of the Nazarenes were surprised by his declaration of greatness: "All bare him witness, and wondered at the gracious words which proceeded out of his mouth. And they said, Is not this Joseph's son?" (V. 22.) They knew Jesus as the local carpenter's son and could not see Him as the Son of God. They were blinded to the divinity within Him because of the humanity that surrounded them.

Masterworks around Us

How many of us fail to see the masterworks around us because we have not yet discovered the worth within ourselves—and within all people? If we stop believing in our own and in each other's abilities, we are implying that we (and all people) are incapable of improvement, beyond change, and essentially without worth. Our thoughts and actions may be undermining the very belief to which we adhere. In fact, the failure to believe in each other's possibilities for change and improvement is one of the most subtle but penetrating forms of judgment—and one of the most unforgiving paradigms we can have.

As simple and even as "Sunday schoolish" as it may sound, when we remember that we and all of our associates are children of God, we will find it easier to surmount our interpersonal problems, to deepen our understanding, broaden our mental and emotional horizons, and change our limiting paradigms. C. S. Lewis reminds us of the extraordinariness of each of us, and of the divinity within us: "There are no ordinary people. You have never talked to a mere mortal. Nations, cultures, arts, civilizations—these are mortal, and their life is to ours as the life of a gnat. But it is immortals whom we joke with, work with, marry, snub, and exploit—immortal horrors or everlasting splendors."

No matter how abundant our attitude and how accepting our love, we all experience a certain amount of empowering splendor when we stop to realize that there really are no ordinary people! All family members, friends, neighbors, associates, and even strangers are children of God, immortal heirs of a divine endowment of worth. This truth alone can cause us to evaluate our interpersonal habits and to work at making our thoughts and actions more accurate reflections of such an understanding.

It becomes a lot more difficult to hold a grudge against someone who is not just a boss or a friend or an associate but also a brother or sister in God's family. It is harder to be resentful of another's abilities and successes when we realize that those abilities are developed, God-given endowments. Differences of opinion can become less threatening when we remind ourselves of the overriding similarity we all have as children of God — when we recall and make claim to the unchanging worth that surpasses our human misunderstandings.

We will find it more natural to focus on others instead of ourselves when we have charity and sincerely look for the sculptures in the stones, the masterpieces around us and within us.

CHAPTER 13

FOCUSING ON OTHERS

One thing I know: the only ones among you who will truly be happy are those who have sought and found how to serve.

— Albert Schweitzer

If we have really internalized the belief that we are children of God, we will ascribe that same belief to all people. We cannot fully realize our God-given worth if we do not simultaneously acknowledge the divine birthright of all of God's children. But sometimes we suffer from the "mirror malady," the self-inflicted condition of seeing only ourselves and our own needs. As we go through life with a mirror in front of us, we may think we see ourselves as the child of God who we are. But until we can look away from the mirror—into the faces of other people—and still see the same picture of worth, we have not fully caught sight of our divine character.

Just as our *intra*personal discussions on self-worth aimed at taking the "self" out of self-improvement, our worth-inspired suggestions for *inter*personal relations will help us improve the quality of our lives by focusing on others. When we find something that brings us greater happiness or fulfillment, we naturally want to share it with others. And this principle applies to our divine connection. When we have a deep sense of our own worth, one of the first things we desire is to help others discover their infinite worth. The joy of our own enlightenment is compounded by the happiness and purpose we help others to achieve.

Pay Value to Others

An effective way to guide others to this greater understanding of their worth is to show them appreciation, or to pay value to them. Psychologist William James said, "The deepest principle of human nature is the craving to be appreciated." When we let other people know that their efforts, sacrifices, and improvements are noticed, we remind them of their inherent value to us — and to God. By pausing to appreciate, we stop to say, "You matter to me," "Your efforts are worthwhile," "Your goodness is remarkable," and perhaps most important, "You are demonstrating the divinity within you." When we sincerely appreciate others, we reassure them of their inherent worth.

Unfortunately, most people suffer from what Ruth Stafford Peale calls "appreciation starvation," a deficient supply of grateful recognitions. Many of us go for days, months, and even years without really being thanked — or sometimes even noticed. I learned an important lesson about this from a conscientious and diligent hotel employee who helped me set up for a training seminar I was conducting in Austin, Texas. He was in charge of the set-up and catering, and, as part of his job, he regularly checked to make sure everything was just as it should be in our meeting room. He was responsive to my needs and cheerful about conducting his duties. After the seminar was over, I sent him a brief note thanking him for his excellent services.

I soon received a letter from him in return. He wrote, "I have worked at this hotel for many years, and not once have I ever received a note from anybody thanking me for what I'm paid to do. This is my job. I just wanted you to know I appreciate your giving me that little note thanking me." In all of the years he had worked there, no one had ever thanked him (in writing) for his services! Yet it required so little of my time and energy to write that simple note.

This experience reminds us of the importance — and of the fulfillment — that comes from paying value to others. We all seem to have lower self-esteem than we should have. We all need to hear more positive feedback than we do. And, paradoxically, when we forget about our own needs long enough to sincerely appreciate others and reinforce their positive efforts, we somehow have our needs filled. I did not write the thank-you note to the hotel employee so I would receive a note in return. But I certainly felt better — about myself and life in general — for having done so. (I am always surprised by how many notes I get, thanking me for my thank-you notes!)

Worth-inspired interpersonal appreciation is always reciprocal. Whether the reciprocity comes in the form of another thank-you note or in the warm feeling that accompanies selfless service, in the gesture of appreciation we pay value to ourselves and ultimately to God. The Savior Himself proclaimed, "Inasmuch as ye have done it unto one of the least of these my brethren, ye have done it unto me."

(Matthew 25:40.) Whenever we serve each other by paying value, or by demonstrating appreciation, we are also honoring Him who endowed us with infinite value and unchanging worth. We thank God by thanking His children.

Once we start looking for opportunities to serve others by paying value, we will find them all around us: in the grocery store, at the bank, in the office, in our neighborhood, across the extended family, and in our own homes. When someone bags our groceries in just the right way, deposits our check with efficiency, unselfishly helps with an important work assignment, watches our home while we are away, sends us an article about a distant relative, or cleans the kitchen without being asked, we can—and should—pay value to them by sincerely thanking them. Sometimes more than a verbal expression of gratitude, a written "thank-you" shows real appreciation and allows us to read and re-read our positive reassurances.

Have you ever noticed how hard it is to throw such a note away? We all tend to hold on to these notes from long ago, file them away among our earthly treasures, and internalize their messages. Once when I presented this idea in a seminar, a woman in the middle of the room started waving a note back and forth like a flag. She was causing such a stir that I stopped speaking for a moment to find out why everyone was staring in her direction. When I saw the note in her hand, I asked her if she would share it with the rest of us. She said that she and her daughter had not been seeing eye to eye. After their extended disagreement, her daughter had given her this note of apology and appreciation. Their argument had taken place six years before our meeting, yet the woman still carried the note in her purse, read it regularly, and was uplifted by its message! The note was just a few lines long, but it meant so much to a sensitive mother.

Two-Minute-Single-Stamp Program

Such a simple investment in another person continues to produce priceless dividends. Our appreciation notes need not take more than two minutes of our time and a single stamp, but their effects will be well worth that small bit of energy and expense. I call this the two-minute-single-stamp program for interpersonal success. And I can attest to the fact that it works! I have a friend who wrote me a note every month for well over a year encouraging me to continue work on this book. Every month I could count on receiving a motivational message from this person, inspiring me to keep writing and letting me know how anxious she was to read my book. Her short notes were encouraging, and her simple way of paying value was most meaningful to me.

Small, simple acts have great consequences. I am always amazed by how much a warm smile can do, how far an inspirational word can lead, and how motivating an encouraging touch can be. Why do such apparently insignificant things mean so much? Perhaps because they give us tangible demonstrations of our otherwise intangible worth. Our understanding of the worth within us becomes more clear as we focus on others and help them discover the very worth we may ourselves be struggling to recover. When we look away from the mirror and into the glass of another's world, we are able to see our own reflection of worth. Only then does the Lord's light shine through us and highlight the divinity within us.

Little Things Matter

A common roadblock to serving others is the perception that our service has to be of impressive proportions — on a grand scale. But as marriage counselor Carlfred Broderick points out in *Marriage and the Family,* the "little" services we render are perhaps most effective in building another's sense of worth:

> Both research and experience show us there are many things one can do directly to help increase a partner's sense of worth. Some techniques are so well known that it is almost embarrassing to recount them here: a compliment, a nondemanding touch, an appreciative look, a smile. Perhaps one might add remembering important things, avoiding hurtful or sensitive areas, and paying attention when the other person is talking. Yet despite the almost universal awareness of the power and value of these gestures, they are missing altogether from many relationships and exceeding rare in many more.[1]

In the interpersonal relationship of marriage or in any other relationship, the same principles of service apply. When we serve others because we want to demonstrate how much they mean to us, it hardly matters what form our service may take. The service itself is not as important as the motive behind that service. We serve because we value their friendship, support, effort, example, love, and association — because they are of worth to us.

Unfortunately, however, we sometimes think that we cannot serve others unless our service makes a life-changing difference and significantly contributes to others' well-being. But that is not true. A prosperous and prominent businessman is well known for the money he donates to universities, hospitals, charities, and homeless shelters. His wealth has been estimated at $450 million, yet he first started sharing his earnings when he was making only $222 a month as a Navy ensign. Recalling those early years, he says, "We would give a certain percentage to those on the ship who were struggling — and we got through life very fine in those days." He gave of his earnings before he had excess funds to give. The joy he experiences now is no greater than the joy he felt when giving to others meant sharing only a few dollars each month. Service does not need to cost a lot in terms of monetary goods; it just needs to come from the heart — not always from the pocketbook. Because we do not have to be rich or powerful to effectively serve or give, the money does not matter nearly so much as the motive for our service.

The Widow's Mite

The Lord taught such a lesson when He "sat over against the treasury, and beheld how the people cast money into the treasury: and many that were rich cast in much. And there came a certain poor widow, and she threw in two mites, which make a farthing." (Mark 12:41–42.) Jesus noticed the widow and called His disciples together that He might teach them a lesson from her donation. He explained, "This poor widow hath cast more in, than all they which have cast into the treasury: for all they did cast in of their abundance; but she of her want did cast in all that she had, even all her living." (Vv. 43–44.) She gave *all* of her money to the Lord because she valued Him and His gospel more than "even all her living."

To fully appreciate the meaning of this account, it helps to know just how much (or how little) a mite was worth. A mite was the smallest bronze coin used by the Jews, and, as the scripture notes, two mites made a farthing. It took sixteen farthings to make a denarius, or penny. So, from a monetary perspective, the widow's contribution was insignificant—literally next to nothing.

But from Jesus' greater understanding, the widow's mite was beyond monetary measure. She had given freely, from her heart, with the pure intent of showing respect and love to the Lord. She was not giving to flaunt her own worthiness or "to be seen of men" but rather to recognize the worth of those who would be the beneficiaries of the treasury.

Modern versions of this story take place in quiet ways all around us. A successful businessman was waiting for a ride at a street corner in Salt Lake City when a panhandler approached and asked if the man could spare a quarter. The businessman literally had empty pockets at the time and pulled both of his pant pockets inside-out so the inquirer could witness his present poverty. And then a tender, beautifully human interaction took place. The vagrant reached into his own pocket and pulled out a dime. He turned to the businessman and sincerely said, "Maybe you will need this more than I will today." The businessman gently refused the offer, the panhandler went on his way, and both were touched by the spirit of giving. While there were many attitudinal and economic differences between the two, this moment seemed to witness to both of them that there was a connection between them — and between all mankind — even a divine connection. They were on equal standing because they were equally willing to give, to pay value to each other by sharing of themselves and by affirming each others' worth.

As Mother Teresa has said, "Do small things with great love." Or as the poet Wordsworth has written, "That best portion of a good man's life / [Is] his little, nameless, un-remembered, acts / Of kindness and love." Whether the services we perform are anonymous or clearly identifiable, whenever we extend kindness and love to others we enjoy "that best portion of a good man's life."

Often small and almost habitual acts of service can bring us more fulfillment than many of the more visible and celebrated contributions. I know a woman who frequently leaves work a few minutes early so she can check the parking meters near her office building and put money in those that have expired. She walks along the curbside and puts loose change in the meters, getting a special thrill from helping people she does not even know and who will probably never even realize she helped them. Kind acts have become so much a part of her character that she is simply in the habit of helping others in her own quiet, anonymous way. I have joked with her about giving her life's savings to a parking meter, and she has been quick to respond, "It only costs me a few cents a day, and I feel great for weeks after. It's the best investment I could ever make with that money."

The Snowball Effect

I have been on the other side of such anonymous service, and I know how affirming such thoughtful gestures can be. I recall getting ready to go to work one morning after a heavy snowstorm, expecting my car and driveway to be buried in snow. To my surprise, someone had already swept the snow from my car and shoveled my driveway. This simple, thoughtful gesture was so meaningful to me. I never found out who did it, but I knew that someone was thinking about me. In a small and yet personalized way, I knew that I mattered.

Even if that person did not know my name and could not recognize my face, I was touched by someone's caring attitude — about me specifically and about people in general. My worth was affirmed by another's thoughtfulness, and, as a result, I looked for an opportunity that day — and for days thereafter — to affirm someone else's worth, to build another's self-esteem by returning an anonymous favor.

The effects of one simple act of service are immeasurable. One favor leads to another — and then to another. One affirmation of worth builds another's esteem, and then that person is in a better position to recognize someone else's worth — and so on. Worth-validating service has a "snowballing effect." Greater than any of the actual services we provide, paying value to each other through those acts is the more meaningful thing we do. When we take a moment of time, a portion of our goods, an ounce of our energy to lighten others' loads and alleviate their burdens, we serve not only by helping but most of all by recognizing each other's worth.

Are You Listening?

One of the most affirming recognitions of worth we can extend is a listening ear. No matter how many plates of cookies we may bring, how many leaves we may rake, and how many dishes we may wash, if we do not take time to serve by listening, our other efforts to help will not be as worthwhile. Listening is an especially important form of service because it is a direct affirmation of another's worth. By closing our own mouths and letting another person talk, we are, in effect, saying that we value what that other person thinks and says. We care enough to put our own thoughts and feelings in the background while someone else has the conversational foreground.

Certainly such listening takes courage. We may hear things that we do not want to hear. We may disagree with what the other person is saying. But we will invariably learn more about ourselves and other people if we stop talking and start listening. As the old proverb advises, "There is no one so deaf as he or she who will not listen." And as the Lord Himself implored, "He that hath ears to hear, let him hear." (Luke 8:8.) We have all been given two ears and only one mouth. Maybe this is a message from our Creator to each of us: we should listen twice as much as we speak!

Hearing is a faculty; listening is a skill. No matter how well we may *hear*, we can become better *listeners* than we are right now. In fact, those of us who think we need no improvement in listening probably have the greatest need to sharpen our listening skills.

A good place to start acquiring these skills is by observing people close to you whom you consider to be excellent listeners. Those people probably always seem to ask the right questions, rephrase what they have been told, and check to see that they are understanding. They will use open-ended questions that require more than a one-word reply and "what," "how," and "why" questions that lend themselves to more discovery and explanation. Good listeners "play back" feelings or rephrase what someone is telling them. They also pause to make sure that they understand what someone has been saying.

Let's consider some of the traits of a poor listener. Four recurring roadblocks to effective listening are "debating," "detouring," "jumping ahead," and "private planning." And each pitfall merits careful scrutiny:

1. *Debating.* We debate when we disagree with someone. Even if we have a valid point, sometimes we do not allow the other person to fully express himself or herself because we interrupt with our own contending viewpoint. If we will just wait and hear the other person out, we may find that we have less of a difference of opinion than we initially thought.

2. *Detouring.* We detour when we change the subject. Have you ever tried to talk to someone, only to have the person start talking about something else? It becomes increasingly frustrating to express yourself when the person with whom you are speaking insists on changing the subject. Neither topic of conversation (the speaker's nor the listener's) gets fully addressed when detouring disturbs our listening.

3. *Jumping ahead.* The average rate of speech is around 125 words a minute. But we are capable of listening and comprehending at speeds of 500 to 600 words a minute. We can all listen a lot faster than we can speak, so people often jump ahead and make conclusions about what the speaker is saying before everything has been said. In the meantime, the listener may be mistaken about the speaker's conclusion and may also muddle what is presently being said.

4. *Private planning.* Even while we exhibit all of the outward gestures of effective listening, we may inwardly be formulating our next response or quietly organizing the rest of the day's activities. Someone may be telling us one thing while we are privately considering other ideas or planning for alternate activities. Private planning can be a plague to effective listening because it busies our minds with irrelevant and distracting thoughts.

Regardless of how savvy we are in the latest listening skills, if we are motivated by anything less than genuine concern and real interest, if we listen with anything less than a worth-inspired empathy, our listening abilities will be inhibited. We will always be less attentive than we could be and less responsive than we should be when a recognition of the speaker's worth and an understanding of the speaker's feelings does not guide our interest. When we wholeheartedly understand that we are not just listening to our spouse, a boss, a neighbor, a friend, or a sibling and instead remind ourselves that the person is also a member of God's family, we will more readily give him or her the respect and attention that is their God-given birthright — and our familial responsibility and privilege.

No Man Is an Island

We are all in this together. Whether we are carrying on a conversation, driving a car, eating in a restaurant, making a business transaction, or getting a permit to build our own home, we cannot get away from the reality of our connectedness as human beings. Every day we are "forced" to rely upon and trust people, from our close friends and family to the complete strangers in our life. Every time we get in the car, our safe journey is dependent upon other drivers' skills as much as upon our own driving techniques. Each time we fly in an airplane, we are, in a sense, turning our lives over to the pilot and flight crew. Even when we eat canned or processed food, we are trusting in the fact that those who have packaged and prepared it have done so in such a way that it is safe for us to eat.

It is probably impossible to go through a day without putting our trust in the products or services of other human beings.

Life is by nature *inter*personal. We are all interdependent components of one great whole. Philosopher and poet John Donne explained this phenomenon centuries ago in his famous creed in "Devotions XVII": "No man is an island, entire of itself; every man is a piece of the continent, a part of the main; if a clod be washed away by the sea, Europe is the less, as well as if a promontory were, as well as if a manor of thy friends or of thine own were; any man's death diminishes me, because I am involved in mankind; and therefore never send to know for whom the bell tolls; it tolls for thee."

Just as all the parts of the earth—the islands, the seas, the continents, the heavens—come together to form one great planet, all of the people on earth compose one great family. With God as our Father, we are all brothers and sisters, working individually and collectively to achieve the best possible lives. And when we give credence to this most important interpersonal relationship, we better understand how all of our thoughts, actions, and daily interactions— no matter how apparently insignificant—ultimately affect our way of life. The more we contribute to the great whole of humanity by losing ourselves in the service of others, the more satisfying and fulfilling all of our interpersonal relationships will become. The sooner we accept this human interdependence as a divinely inspired condition for personal improvement, the more fully we will take advantage of the refinement that comes from "having" to get along with other people.

At some point, all of us have probably contemplated moving far away, escaping all of our troubles, becoming a hermit. We may have thought to ourselves how controlled, kind, and sensitive we would be if we could just do things in our own way on our own schedule. We would be such a loving parent if only we could escape our parenthood for a while. We would be a much better employee if only we had the office to ourselves for several days. We would be a more sensitive friend if only our neighbors would not call every day—hour after hour. We would be a more courteous and patient driver if no one else were on the road. We would be a more pleasant spouse if only our husband or wife knew when to leave us alone. And yet, none of us really likes the thought of being totally alone. We seem to want other people — but perhaps on our own terms.

But an entirely different and more demanding sort of development takes place when our personal progress is so intertwined with others' lives — when we must adjust our personal expectations and desires to comply with others' pressing needs. For this very reason of interdependence, just recognizing our own worth is not enough. In fact, we cannot fully realize our worth unless we also recognize that all human beings are beneficiaries of that same God-given value.

Three A's of Interpersonal Success

Once we make this multilateral commitment to becoming a better person and focusing on others, the three A's of interpersonal success (which we have discussed throughout this section without labeling them as such) will fall more naturally into our hearts, minds, and actions:

1. Acceptance
2. Appreciation
3. Attention

The first A, *acceptance* of others, refers to avoiding judgment, loving unconditionally, and forgiving trespasses. The second A, *appreciation* for others, is demonstrated when we believe in and verbalize their inherent abilities and capabilities. And the third A, *attention,* is the subject of this chapter: paying value to each other by serving, listening, and, in general, focusing on others instead of ourselves.

The Lord's Fold

In spite of our differences of race, color, and creed, we are all sheep in the Lord's fold. We are all of equal and unchanging worth to the Master Shepherd. When the Lord explained, "My sheep hear my voice, and I know them, and they follow me," He did not mean that some sheep (or people) could not be in His fold. (John 10:27.) He simply explained our relationship to God in terms of agency. He preceded this description with the explanation, "I told you, and ye believed not." (V. 25.) Many of us who do not know the Lord or hear His voice have chosen not to accept our relationship to Him: perhaps we do not believe He is our mediator with the Father or we do not accept our own infinite and inherent worth — as well as the worth of others.

In other words, the lost sheep are those of us who refuse to believe (of their own free will) that they are part of Christ's saving fold. They separate *themselves* from the Lord and ultimately from their brother and sister sheep because they have not made a divine connection to personal worth. The Lord does not separate or leave us; we separate ourselves from Him. In *All These Things Shall Give Thee Experience*, Elder Neal A. Maxwell writes of those who erroneously think God withdraws from them:

> To those who mean well but thoughtlessly speak of 'building a better relationship' with God (which sounds like a transaction between mortals desiring reciprocity), it needs to be said that our relationship with God is already established, in a genealogical sense. Perhaps what such individuals intend to say is that we must draw closer to God.[2]

By virtue of our birth — our eternal genealogy — we are already a member of the Lord's fold. And since the beginning of time, He has invited all of His sheep to graze in the rich and fertile pasture of righteous living. If we should choose to sample the terrain in other pastures and take the risk of becoming wayward, it is not the Lord who loses sight of us. We lose sight of His eternal rewards for us and follow our own less-fulfilling and rockier way.

Lost sheep often see themselves as independently worthy, not needing Christ's recompense; or they see themselves as worthless, unworthy to be succored by His stewardship. In both cases, they are self-serving and thereby self-centered. As a result, they do not fully realize their God-given worth because they close their ears to His voice, separate themselves from His guidance, and shut themselves off from the sustaining support of their brother and sister sheep.

But when we sincerely lose ourselves in the service of others, when we improve our interpersonal relationships by taking the "self" out of self-improvement, we will find ourselves in the comfort and warmth of the Lord's saving embrace.

Upon these precepts hinge all of the self-improvement theories advanced in this book. Just as the personal is not without the interpersonal, both personal and interpersonal improvement will not take place unless a deep and abiding understanding of our interdependent nature and God-given worth motivates these efforts. And in the process, both our own and others' needs, desires, and expectations will be met.

THE ABUNDANT LIFE

We have inherent power and purpose.
The deep sense of hope and humility
that comes from recognizing our self-worth
will lead to a more abundant life.

CHAPTER 14

LIVING WITH POWER AND PURPOSE

No doubt the Lord God could have made life easy for us all if such had been His plan and purpose. He could so have surrounded us, could so have provided, that we could have lived all but effortlessly. But He has given us something infinitely greater than an effortless existence. He has given us eternal principles, freedom, the right to work, the right to learn (even the right to make mistakes if we must), the right to fail — and the incentive to succeed, with glorious promises and privileges and possibilities.

— Richard L. Evans

We are not pawns on a celestial chessboard, randomly put here, tossed about, and expected to figure out for ourselves the "game" of life. We have purpose, destiny, and reason for being. The very world in which we live manifests the purposefulness of all of God's creations. Just as every plant, insect, fish, and animal has a unique and individualized role in the earth's ecosystem, every human being has God-given abilities that enable him or her to make distinctive contributions to humanity: to be a purposeful player in life's many arenas. And the more we realize our worth — and with that, the worth of all of God's children — the more fully we will discover our purpose in the ecosystem of eternity. We will better be able to make correct choices, fulfill worthy expectations, and meet divinely inspired goals. A recognition of our own and others' self-worth gives us personal (and interpersonal) power as well as Godly purpose.

Power and Purpose

The first three sections of the book addressed the relationship between God-given worth and personal power. We explored how an understanding of our eternal relationship with our Heavenly Father could not only change the way we see ourselves but also alter our expectations for ourselves. The fourth section of the book advanced the truth that personal power is not really efficacious unless it also has interpersonal purpose, or godly influence in the lives of others.

These two blessings, power and purpose, give us the ability to endure life's challenges and to empathize with those who feel "worth-*less*" or unworthy. When we do so, we begin to develop a reverence and patience for the process of life. We have analyzed specifically how endurance and empathy are direct by-products of realizing our worth. But on a more general level, we have yet to discuss how this recognition allows us to "*live* until we die," to take full advantage of the richness of life. Living abundantly and believing wholeheartedly in our inherent worth are interchangeable descriptions of *real* self-improvement.

An Abundant Life

For me, these descriptions have come to be representative of my mother's abundant orientation toward life. Not much over middle age, Mom experienced what I consider some of the most challenging trials anyone could endure. Within just a few short years, she lost her eternal companion to an industrial accident and underwent major brain surgery. No longer having her loving husband's ready support, she was left to deal with a substantial loss of mobility and other neurological (equilibrium-associated) problems. Essentially stripped of her health and entirely without her husband, she spent a couple of months in the hospital and then returned to an emptier-than-ever home. These less than favorable circumstances could have made her bitter and angry. She easily could have felt as if she were "picked on," punished, or unfairly caused to suffer. But she did not let her trials destroy her inner resolve.

She not only maintained her positive outlook and resilient resolve to improve, but she also became even more grateful for the blessings she did have. Life took on a new preciousness and precariousness. Covered by all of the medical tubes, blankets, and bandages that were sustaining her physical life, she would frequently say things like "Life is so short" and "I'm so grateful to be alive." She reassured us, "Don't be so worried. I'm fine. I'm still alive!" Though her physical problems were serious and pressing, she would daily ask about her grandchildren, her children, their spouses, and even neighbors. Her unselfish concern for others transcended the physical challenges that could have consumed all of her thoughts and energies. She prayed in the horizontal position and looked to the Lord to help her make faith the active principle she knew it to be.

Her condition has not improved overnight. She still struggles physically. But spiritually, she is strong, hopeful, humble, and grateful. She spends much of her day making and taking phone calls, receiving friends and family, and, most of all, offering an empathetic ear, a welcome word, a loving embrace to all who enter. She may not be able to bring a meal to her neighbors, but she always offers them a listening ear. She may not be able to visit her family and friends as she would like, but a steady stream of visitors and loved ones come to draw from her inner strength. She knows that the Lord has a purpose for her, even though that purpose is different from what she had always thought it would be: spending the latter years with her husband, serving missions together, visiting grandchildren together, and enjoying the richness of life—together. Nonetheless, she knows that as a daughter of God, she has great inner power and unchanging worth. And she is determined to use that positive expectancy and faith to lead others to the abundant life she still enjoys.

Abundant living need not come in the form of daily exercise, an hour of reading, a period of meditation, a creative activity, or a weekly escape to nature. Living an abundant life is the result of a complete, abiding, and even transforming understanding of our God-given worth. Whether such a recognition manifests itself by inspiring us to run marathons or to relax and meditate without guilt is not important. There is no one right way to live abundantly.

But recognizing our God-given worth (and acting upon that understanding) is the way to define a uniquely designed, divinely empowered, and abundantly fulfilling life. Living the "good" life means living a child of God's life, or making the most of life's circumstances by designing a life-style that reflects a recognition of our inherent worth.

What We Can Do

But how can we design a truly abundant life if we are still not sure that we have infinite worth? In plain terms, how can we recognize our worth? Perhaps the first step in achieving such a recognition is becoming aware of the *possibility* of realizing such a divine endowment. In large measure, raising our level of awareness has been the object of this book. But on a day-to-day, closed-book level, how can we come to this recognition of God's unconditional and all-encompassing love for us?

The answer to this question begins in many of the self-improvement books that we already love and live by. When we take time to exercise, read, pray, memorize, or meditate, we often feel a sense of accomplishment or worthiness that inspires us to become better and to do more — for ourselves and for others. We must recognize that there is a mind-body-spirit connection. Even if some of the self-improvement we are pursuing does not seem to have any apparent connection to God or spirituality, self-improving is an important step that leads to a realization of our God-given worth. If for no other reason, it makes us feel better about ourselves. And when our self-esteem is in good working order, we are in a better position to internalize the truth that each of us is literally a child of God. Such positive self-esteem and self-improvement leads us to become a better self: a self that is more like the child of God we really are. Just after an exhilarating walk or upon finishing an inspiring chapter or while meditating and praying, we feel a few steps closer to the divinity within us than when otherwise engaged in more distracting activities.

While a recognition of our worth begins with the activities we read about in one improvement book after another, it is not complete until the "self" is taken out of self-improvement—until we look to God and realize that we are not only empowered by Him but that we are also literally dependent upon Him for any lasting progress that we make. Ultimately, we would not be able to change and grow if we were not in the first place created by Him, endowed with eternal worth, and then saved through His Son's atoning sacrifice.

Unfortunately, however, after making some of the initial, popular efforts to self-improve, much of our real, transformational progress is never actualized because of a lack of hope or a shortage of humility.

The Power of Hope

Despite the fact that we all make mistakes, we all can have hope in a better tomorrow. Perhaps the most essential ingredient for personal and interpersonal improvement is the real sense of hope that comes from understanding the gospel of repentance and growth. Hope is the necessary forerunner not only of change but also of abundant living. Samuel Johnson said it well: "It is necessary to hope, . . . for hope itself is happiness."

Without hope, we cannot fully realize who we are or come to understand the well-spring of worth within us. Because we are surrounded by so many situations that are hostile to the human spirit, because so many people and philosophies would have us believe that we are *worthless* (even unable to grow and improve), a deep-seated sense of hope must guide our life and living. We must not mock faith by failing to cultivate its parent Hope — or by not believing in our divinely endowed worth. Because of God's perfect love and forgiveness, we are much more potential than we are actuality. As children of God, we are never hopeless. With His love and hope, we can discover our eternal potential and live the abundant life that is hallmarked by hope.

Although we may get discouraged from time to time and — if only for a moment — believe that we cannot change or improve, we must quickly separate ourselves from our failures and remember that failure is an *event*, never a person. God did not make any failures. Instead, He created changing, growing, developing sons and daughters who can become more like Him. We, with the Psalmist, can say, "In thee, O Lord, do I hope." (Psalm 38:15.) This precious perspective will strengthen our hope as life's lessons refine and define us.

The Power of Humility

Just as hope is essential in the midst of disappointment and despair, so humility is necessary during periods of prosperity. When everything does seem to be going well, when our expectations are met and our goals are achieved, we must give credit where it is rightfully due. If we fail to acknowledge the hand of the Lord in all our successes — even in all our daily and many times seemingly insignificant victories, we are ignoring our God-given worth. If we pat ourselves on the back and glorify our own abilities and achievements, we are relying on false securities to give us strength.

Do we ever base our self-worth on our net worth? I believe we often do. As we seek for the world's goods over the blessings of God, we begin to define our identity by our income. We begin measuring ourselves against others and their possessions, sometimes feeling superior because we have more than they do but at other times feeling inferior because their possessions are greater than ours. Round and round we go, in a never-ending cycle of getting and spending. But the truth is, we can never get enough of what we don't need. All the material possessions the world has to offer will never bring the peace and joy we were meant to experience as children of God. And as God's children, we are worth infinitely more than all our possessions — no matter how wealthy we may be.

The things of this world will not last, and if we build our happiness upon them, what will become of our happiness when they are gone? But if we build our happiness on eternal truths and lasting relationships, the loss (or even the acquisition) of material things will ultimately mean very little. As Jesus taught, "What is a man profited, if he shall gain the whole world, and lose his own soul?" (Matthew 16:26.)

For what price would we sacrifice honesty and integrity? Can we place a monetary value on relationships with family and friends? What would we trade for health and happiness? Can anything in the world replace trust and love?

But some continue to trade their birthright for a mess of pottage. As Albert Einstein said, "It is a mistake often made in this country to measure things by the amount of money they cost." And as Jesus said, "Where your treasure is, there will your heart be also." (Matthew 6:21.) Unless our "treasure" is the teachings of the Spirit, the love of our fellow beings, the things that really matter, our lives may be off balance, measuring the meaningful against the material.

When self-esteem is solely a by-product of accomplishment and success, it rests upon the shaky foundation of human performance — which, as we all know, can change and falter. Muhammad Ali, the legendary heavyweight boxing champion, said, "When you're as great as I am, it's hard to be humble." But he, and each of us, can more accurately say that it is hard *not* to be humble when we realize how *truly great* we are, how infinite our possibilities and how unchanging our worth in the sight of God. Jesus explained the danger of self-congratulation and the blessing of relying on the Lord: "Whosoever shall exalt himself shall be abased; and he that shall humble himself shall be exalted." (Matthew 23:12.)

When our self-esteem is built upon a deep-seated recognition of our self-worth, we can enjoy a steady and encompassing feeling of success and worthiness. Then we can receive the Lord's saving grace and feel His empowering and inspiring arm around our shoulders.

The comforting warmth I felt after my father's death

when I put his sweater over my shoulders came from the deepest sort of humility and heavenward dependence. At a moment in my life when circumstances forced me to find security in no other place than the Lord's peaceful assurance, I was given more inner strength and transformational understanding than ever before. The saving truth expressed by the Apostle Peter became real to me, "All of you be subject one to another, and be clothed with humility: for God resisteth the proud, and giveth grace to the humble. Humble yourselves therefore under the mighty hand of God, that he may exalt you in due time: casting all your care upon him; *for he careth for you.*" (1 Peter 5:5–7; italics added.)

Our Father Lives

Greater than any of the blessings that come from a deeply internalized recognition of our worth is this deep sense of humility. Such meekness and submissiveness to God's will give us the ability to see past our own weaknesses, develop all necessary strengths, and realize our potential. From such God-fearing humility comes the exalting understanding that God *is* our Heavenly Father. And therein lies the power of self-worth and the means for real improvement. This quiet explosion of inner strength is founded on the simple belief that our Father lives. The words of a children's song explain this process well:

> I know my Father lives and loves me too.
> The Spirit whispers this to me and tells me it is true,
> And tells me it is true.
>
> He sent me here to earth, by faith to live his plan.

The spirit whispers this to me and tells me that I can,
And tells me that I can.[1]

Every one of us, adult and child, will say, "I can" when we
come to know that "it is true": our Heavenly Father lives,
loves, and knows us. Every one of us progresses when we
lose ourselves in the service of God by transforming ourselves
through a recognition of our self-worth, by serving others,
realizing that we have purpose to our lives and having
reverence for the divine power within us. I know my Heavenly Father lives. And because of that, I know my earthly
father still lives and that we will meet again someday. I
know there is reason for our being. And I know that each
of us has inherent worth as a child of God. As we make
the divine connection to self-improvement, we can be personally transformed through God's saving and eternal plan
for progress.

NOTES

Preface

1. Jeffrey R. Holland, " 'Mirror, Mirror on the Wall': A Look at the 'Me Decade,' " in *1979 Devotional Speeches of the Year* (Provo, Ut.: Brigham Young University Press, 1980), p. 45.

Chapter 1

1. *Newsweek*, February 17, 1992, p. 48.

2. See *Webster's New Twentieth-Century Dictionary*, unabridged.

3. *Hymns* (Salt Lake City: The Church of Jesus Christ of Latter-day Saints, 1985), no. 301.

Chapter 2

1. James E. Talmage, *Jesus the Christ*, 3rd ed. (Salt Lake City: The Church of Jesus Christ of Latter-day Saints, 1916), pp. 460–61.

2. Dale Carnegie, *How to Stop Worrying and Start Living* (New York: Pocket Books, 1985), pp. 291–93.

3. C. S. Lewis, *Mere Christianity* (New York: Macmillan Publishing Co., 1981), pp. 173–74.

4. In Francis M. Gibbons, *David O. McKay: Apostle to the World, Prophet of God* (Salt Lake City: Deseret Book Co., 1986), p. 288.

Chapter 3

1. Dennis Waitley, *The Double Win* (Old Tappan, N.J.: Fleming H. Revell Co., 1985), p. 119.

2. Dan Coats, "America's Youth: Crisis of Character," *Imprimis*, September 1991, pp. 1–3.

3. "The Retro Campaign," *U.S. News and World Report*, December 9, 1991, p. 32.

4. Ibid.

5. Neal A. Maxwell, *All These Things Shall Give Thee Experience* (Salt Lake City: Deseret Book Co., 1979), p. 47.

6. Napoleon Hill, *Grow Rich with Peace of Mind* (New York: Ballantine Books, 1982), p. 68.

Chapter 4

1. *Think and Grow Rich Newsletter*, January 1991, p. 1.

2. Robert Fulghum, *All I Really Need to Know I Learned in Kindergarten* (New York: Ballantine Books, 1989), p. 116.

3. *U.S. News & World Report*, February 4, 1991, pp. 52–53.

Chapter 5

1. Richard L. Bednar and Scott R. Peterson, *Spirituality and Self-Esteem* (Salt Lake City: Deseret Book Co., 1990), p. 3.

2. Stephen R. Covey, *The 7 Habits of Highly Effective People* (New York: Simon & Schuster, 1989), pp. 18–19.

3. See William D. Hersey, *Blueprints for Memory* (New York: American Management Assoc., 1990), p. 62.

4. In *Richard Evans' Quote Book* (Salt Lake City: Publisher's Press, 1971), p. 65.

Chapter 6

1. See Shad Helmstetter, *The Self-Talk Solution* (New York: William Morrow and Co., 1987).

2. Norman Vincent Peale, *The Power of Positive Thinking* (New York: Fawcett Crest, 1991), pp. 116–17.

3. See David D. Burns, *Feeling Good Handbook* (New York: Penguin Books, 1990), pp. 8–11.

4. Wendell J. Ashton, "Warrior's Wisdom," *Instructor*, September 1963, back cover.

5. *U.S. New and World Report*, July 29, 1991, pp. 43–44.

6. Warren Bennis, "Four Competencies of Great Leaders," in *Empowering Business Resources*, Ken Shelton, ed. (Glenview, Ill.: Scott, Foresman and Co., 1990), p. 208.

7. Lewis, *Mere Christianity*, p. 173.

Chapter 7

1. In Lewis, *Mere Christianity*, p. 171.
2. In *Plus: The Magazine of Positive Thinking*, June 1991, p. 3.
3. In *Richard Evans' Quote Book*, p. 136.
4. Neal A. Maxwell, *Deposition of a Disciple* (Salt Lake City: Deseret Book Co., 1976), p. 29.

Chapter 8

1. Lewis, *Mere Christianity*, p. 178.

Chapter 9

1. Marvin J. Ashton, *Ye Are My Friends* (Salt Lake City: Deseret Book Co., 1982), p. 29.
2. Joseph Campbell, *The Power of Myth*, Betty Sue Flowers, ed. (New York: Doubleday, 1988), p. 193.
3. *Think and Grow Rich Newsletter*, July 1991, p. 8.
4. Lindsey Hall and Leigh Cohn, eds., *Recoveries: True Stories by People Who Conquered Addiction and Compulsion* (Carlsbad, Cal.: Gürze Book Co., 1987), p.141.

Chapter 10

1. Lewis, *Mere Christianity*, p. 183.
2. Charles Dickens, *A Christmas Carol* (London: Octopus Books, 1986), p. 18.
3. *Hymns*, no. 220.
4. Denis Waitley, *Seeds of Greatness* (audio tape) (Chicago: Nightingale-Conant Corp., 1983), tape 3, side 6.
5. Antoine de Sainte-Exupéry, *The Little Prince*, trans. Katherine Woods (New York: Harcourt Brace Jovanovich, 1983), p. 70.
6. Spencer W. Kimball, *Marriage* (Salt Lake City: Deseret Book Co., 1978), pp. 46–47.

Chapter 11

1. Gordon B. Hinckley, "Of You It Is Required to Forgive," *Ensign*, November 1980, p. 62.
2. Nathaniel Hawthorne, *The Scarlet Letter*, in *Norton Anthology of American Literature*, 2nd ed. (New York: W.W. Norton & Co., 1985), pp. 1193–94.

3. Walter Anderson, "My Toughest Struggle," *Guideposts*, November 1989, pp. 30–33.

4. Boyd K. Packer, "Balm of Gilead," *Ensign*, November 1977, p. 60.

5. William Shakespeare, *The Merchant of Venice*, IV, i, 184.

Chapter 12

1. Paul Thompson, "How to Get from Plateau to Peak," in *Empowering Business Resources*, p. 60.

2. Elizabeth Longford, *Wellington: The Years of the Sword* (Panther Press), p. 506.

3. See *Think and Grow Rich Newsletter*, March 1991, p. 4.

4. See Stephen R. Covey, *The 7 Habits of Highly Effective People*, pp. 219–20.

Chapter 13

1. Carlfred Broderick, *Marriage and the Family* (Englewood Cliffs, N.J.: Prentice-Hall, 1979), pp. 187–94.

2. Neal A. Maxwell, *All These Things Shall Give Thee Experience* (Salt Lake City: Deseret Book Co., 1979), p. 3.

Chapter 14

1. *Hymns*, no. 302.

INDEX